Little Adventures in Tokyo

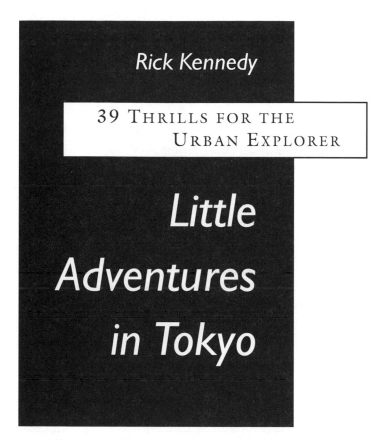

Rick Kennedy

39 THRILLS FOR THE
URBAN EXPLORER

Little

Adventures

in Tokyo

STONE BRIDGE PRESS

Berkeley, California

REVISED, UPDATED EDITION

Published by STONE BRIDGE PRESS
P. O. Box 8208, Berkeley, CA 94707
sbp@stonebridge.com • www.stonebridge.com

The text and maps of this book are based on material
that first appeared in *Tokyo Weekender*.

First edition published 1992

Book design by David Bullen
Maps by Kelly Frankeny

Printed in the United States of America

LIBRARY OF CONGRESS CATALOGING-IN-PUBLICATION DATA
Kennedy, Rick.
    Little adventures in Tokyo: 39 thrills for the urban explorer
/ Rick Kennedy.
        p.   cm.
    ISBN 1-880656-34-5
    1. Tokyo (Japan)—Guidebooks.   I. Title.
    DS896.38.K46   1998
    915.2'1350449—dc21   98-14426
                                                        CIP

CONTENTS

God knows, Tokyo is not a beautiful city. It was built to no plan and it has so few buildings of architectural interest that even a drab pile like Tokyo Station can seem worth preserving.

Various reasons are offered to explain why the Japanese gift for planning and design was somehow never applied to Japan's capital city: the futility of putting up serious buildings on the most earthquake-prone land on earth; the fact that the land in Tokyo is so expensive that any building on that land seems an afterthought; the fact that a great percentage of Tokyo's population doesn't consider Tokyo its hometown (as witness the mass exodus to the provinces during New Year and the summer festival); the fact that in many quarters it is considered immodest to build too grandly; and because in the Japanese way of doing things there is always a large element of laissez-faire.

I suppose there is some truth in each of these rationalizations, but the real reason for Tokyo's being the jumble it is, is that *Tokyoites like it this way.* A talented young Tokyo architect just back from a six-month internship in Washington, D.C., recently told me that she found that city too calculated, too self-aggrandizing, too hard-edged, too predictable. She said she was happy to be back in the cozy confusion of Tokyo, a city where it is impossible to imagine that a concourse could take precedence over people and where every time she turned a corner she expected the unexpected.

You will know that you are beginning to look at the city the way a Tokyoite does when you note the following with pleasure:

- a particularly complex tangle of wires, cables, and junction boxes on a telephone pole.

- a building six stories high and two meters wide painted lime green and hot pink.
- a sign constituting the whole facade of a 500-seat pachinko parlor composed of 25,000 light bulbs and at least ten linear kilometers of crazily flickering neon.
- a little *yakitori* place in a gently sagging, never-been-painted wooden structure right next to the tracks of the Yamanote Line. The building shakes with every passing train and every single one of its panes of glass is cracked. (In a Tokyo context, such a building has *character*.)
- an ivy-covered police box with a clutch of geraniums growing out of a styrofoam carton at the door.
- a putting green on the grounds of an ancient temple, with benches for spectators or people with time on their hands.
- a coffeehouse next to an off-track betting parlor, where everyone without exception is buried in a racing sheet.
- a tea shop which wheels its antique roasting apparatus outside when the weather is fine and so suffuses the whole street with a sweet fragrance (the subtlest advertisement imaginable).

As you get to know Tokyo you will see how its rhythms are different from those of other cities. The acoustics of the city are miraculous: one street over from a busy thoroughfare, it will be as tranquil as a small town. There are hundreds of tiny, tiny parks, sometimes with a carp pool, very often with a solitary swing or slide or seesaw. There are drink vending machines everywhere, often on all four corners of an intersection. Large chunks of the city are still rural, with rice paddies and scarecrows and thickets of green bamboo. Because there is essentially no zoning, you are apt to come across a metalworking shop next to a store selling elegant silk kimono next to a billiard parlor next to a cram school next to a private dwelling next to a public bath. In most of the city, it is impossible to fix a label like "high class" or "low class" to a neighborhood—the neighborhood just is. Every Tokyo alley is cluttered with bicycles. Cats are everywhere, as are crows, the irrepressible city bird.

Tokyo is a city of neighborhoods where everybody knows everybody and there is a strong community feeling. Every neighborhood has its police box, its fishmonger, its saké shop, its unbelievably cluttered little hardware store, its newspaper delivery agent. Most shops are very small: stores so large that the shopkeeper does not know the names of his customers are seen to be lacking in humanity. Every neighborhood has its summer festival with dancing to the thump of a drum and the tootle of a flute and concessions like fishing for goldfish. On New Year's Eve, the neighborhood will gather around a bonfire at the local temple and drink saké donated by the local merchants. In lots of neighborhoods, children appointed to the task will make the rounds of the houses in the evening calling out *"Hi no yojin"*—"Be careful of fire."

I wrote this book because I think Tokyo is a wonderful city and I enjoy showing it off. It's true that a good way to get a feel for the city is simply to walk its winding streets, observing the shop signs ("Perfect Kiss" is an apt name for a shop selling tennis racquets, don't you think?) and the little rituals of living (watch the drill when a car drives into a gas station)—but I want to point you to some special things that you might not run across on your own, because after all, the city is *huge*.

My idea is to take you to a particular place, fill you in on the background of what's happening, and tell you what you should look for and what you should expect. You should be able to negotiate most of these little adventures without knowing any Japanese.

Tokyo is a very safe city. At night it becomes quiet the way New York never does. It is certainly crowded—in front of Shibuya Station 600 people can step off the curb to cross the street when the light changes —but it's easy to find solitude, too. The city is not so driven as New York. There are places to sit down. Coffee shops abound. Public conveniences are for the most part clean and handy. No, Tokyo is not beautiful, but it's got energy and a gritty sort of character and a nutty diversity. To me, that's what urban civilization is all about. On top of all this, you have a chance to watch a major world city being built, for Tokyo is still very much under construction. I hope as you make your way through this book you get a sense of the special qualities of this city.

TOKYO NOW: Another Look

The first edition of *Little Adventures in Tokyo* was published in those heady days when it was calculated that the land occupied by the Imperial Palace near Tokyo Station was worth as much as all the land in California with all the buildings on that land thrown in. Shortly thereafter the overheated Japanese economy hit the wall, but the crazy momentum was such that Tokyo continued to build right on through the downturn.

Tokyu Corporation remodeled most of the stations along the Toyoko Line between Tokyo and Yokohama *without stopping the trains.* Other lines were extended, new stations opened up on existing lines, and there was talk of constructing an underground expressway between the Ginza and Shinjuku, which would be the equivalent of running a tunnel the length of Manhattan.

A brace of splendid new hotels went up, along with Tokyo's first city hall, a building some thought recalled the excesses of Mussolini. Landmark Tower, Japan's tallest building, towered over the Yokohama waterfront, its head often in the clouds. Tama New Town and Kohoku New Town, huge planned communities—a new concept for Tokyo—filled out at a furious pace. There were plans to build American-style shopping malls with hectares and hectares of parking, and the perennial plan to move the government outside the city continued to be agonized over.

In one miraculous year, two sparkling new opera houses opened at opposite ends of town.

By some measures, the quality of life has improved. Tower Records installed Tokyo's first international newsstand of any scale, where newspapers like the *Irish Times* and the *New York Observer* and magazines like *Saveur* (in French) and *Graphis* from Switzerland are for sale. Dozens of sidewalk cafes like Les Bacchanales and Café des Près have sprung up, and not just on the fashionable boulevards. Italian restaurants proliferate. Levain in Tomigaya is baking fine country loaves daily, and discount stores have brought the price of imported wine for daily drinking way down.

But Tokyo remains the funky old city it has always been. It is still hard to find a place to park a bicycle at the station. The crows are still incorrigible. The little drinking places continue to flourish against all economic logic. The trains are still crowded, although flex-time is relieving some of the pressure.

Tokyo continues to be an extraordinary urban landscape, the only city in the world with an active volcano within city limits. I reckon I'll stay.

Rick Kennedy presides over Tokyo Q,
an on-line Tokyo city magazine, at
http://www.so-net.or.jp/tokyoq/.

PART ONE *Old Tokyo*

Tokyo is as old as, say, Boston, Massachusetts—which in Japanese terms is not old at all. To the rest of the country, Tokyo is an upstart city which just happens to be the focal point of Japanese art, music, government, finance, education, publishing, printing, shipping, advertising, communications, and business, as well as being the seat of His Imperial Majesty, who has his own private railway station next to Harajuku Station. A quarter of the population of Japan lives within 50 kilometers of the bridge in downtown Tokyo called Nihonbashi.

But as a large portion of Tokyo's population thinks of "real home" as being somewhere else, the concept "Old Tokyo" has a tinny ring to it.

Still, Old Tokyo does exist and is certainly more alive than Old New York or Olde London, because there was about it from the beginning nothing contrived, nothing unnatural. The face of Old Tokyo is still reflected in the city's gardens, in its temples, its crafts, its old-time eating establishments which haven't changed at all, its traditional festivals, and in the faces of the people on its streets.

Scent Games: The *Kohdo* Ritual

Ready for something really exotic? If you have come to Japan hoping to take away with you an experience of a different category, something without the dull ring of a Japan cliché, something steeped in ancient tradition, something with a bit of a cachet—well, this is it.

Kohdo, the ritual appreciation of incense, is a rarefied aesthetic cult. *Kohdo* (*koh* means "incense" and *do* means "way of knowledge") first appears in Japanese literature in the 11th century, but is pretty clearly even older than that. *Sado*, the tea ceremony, derives much of its ritual from *kohdo*. As *kohdo* is now actively practiced by only a few hundred people in all of Japan, it is an exceedingly esoteric pastime, but at the same time a very accessible one: all you need is a sense of smell.

Those schooled in *kohdo* have seized this sense, which we all take more or less for granted, and raised it to a scarcely credible level of discrimination. An experienced practitioner of *kohdo* can recognize *and put a name to* several hundred scents. There are altogether about six hundred scents in the *koh* pantheon, but many of these are so rare (and so expensive—top-class *koh* is ounce for ounce more expensive than gold) that they might as well no longer exist.

Although *kohdo* is hardly a proselytizing discipline, essentially because good *koh* is so scarce, you are sure to be invited to join a *kohdo* practice session. Only remember not to wear perfume or flowers and not to have recently drunk coffee or eaten garlic, and not to wear rings or a necklace, because they might accidentally strike against the cup bearing the incense, causing a small distraction.

Having made contact with one of the teachers listed at the end of this explanation, present yourself on the appointed hour at the designated classroom and take one of the sheets of paper which sets out the form the session's exercise will take.

As this will comprise a passage of classical Japanese literature written in the flowing hand of Sanjounishi-sensei's wife and what appears to be an alchemical formula, it will probably make little sense. Don't worry: no one will expect you to understand and you will be given a seat near someone who will lead you through the ritual. Proceed by dutiful imitation, just as you would follow the proceedings at an unfamiliar religious service by watching your neighbor out of the corner of your eye.

Everyone at the class will have known each other for years, so the talk around the table before the session starts is the relaxed chatter of friends. In the corner of the room several of the more experienced people will be heating the small charcoal cylinders called *tadon* which when glowing will be buried in the ashes of pond lily seeds, so chosen for their odorlessness and color when reduced to this fine powder.

After the *tadon* is buried in the ashes in a cup (which itself can be an object of veneration, as in the tea ceremony), an intricate pattern is made in the surface of the ashes to reflect not only the season but also give a hint of the form of the contest to come.

Meanwhile at the head of the table, the *Koh* Master for the session readies her equipment. There are seven tools—a small set of pincers called *gingyobasami*, a poker, a set of chopsticks, two spade-like implements, and a feather from the wing of a crested ibis (to brush away any stray ash from the side of the cup).

A small tray with folded strips of Japanese paper is passed around the table. Bow to your neighbor, take one of the slips of paper, write your name on it, and set it in front of your place. Later you will write your answers on it. The session's Record Keeper is busy inscribing by brush the names of the attendants on a large sheet of Japanese paper on which everyone's answers will eventually be recorded, right or wrong, for everyone to see.

The *Koh* Master announces, *"Koh hajimemasu"* ("The *koh* ceremony will begin") and proceeds, in a manner which recalls the tea ceremony, to fold a napkin, wipe the *gingyobasami*, and lay her implements gracefully down on the pad of paper before her, making the absolute minimum of noise. In the room now, dead silence. For the next 40 minutes or so, only the *Koh* Master will speak, and then only sparingly, as dictated by the ritual.

The *Koh* Master opens a box containing ten small squares of quartz, which she arranges on a wooden holder. Using her *gingyobasami*, she carefully places one of the quartz squares on top of the pattern of ashes in a cup, over the burning charcoal.

She then unwraps the first piece of *koh*, a piece of wood naturally saturated with fragrant oils, a gift of nature only as large as the paring of a fingernail—and places it on top of the quartz, which is beginning to heat up. After a few moments, the *Koh* Master lifts the cup to her nose and, cupping her left hand over the cup to focus the scent, "listens" to the fragrance. (In the vocabulary of *kohdo*, the verb "to smell" is *kiku*, which in everyday Japanese means "to listen.") If the *Koh* Master judges the koh to be giving off scent properly, she will pass the cup to the person on her right, announcing, *"Kokoromi ichi de gozaimasu"* ("This is the first test scent").

The most common form the *koh* contest takes is for the *Koh* Master first to pass around the table one or more "test" scents, after which three or more "real" scents *(hon koh)* are passed around. The participants must then identify these real scents as being the same as a particular test scent or as being a ringer, not one of the test scents at all. The contest can be fiendish, as all the *hon koh* to be identified might be the same *koh* or, equally as deceptive, all might be ringers.

There are formally more than 2,000 forms a *koh* contest can take, some of wondrous complexity with the answer required to be given in the form of a haiku composed on the spot. Mind games soon become part of the matching of scents, as the mind naturally tries to discriminate between very subtle differences, searching for a connection between some deliciously fragrant *koh* from the outside ring of a tree and a *koh* from nearer the core of the same tree. Are they the same *koh* or are they different?

Charcoal heated to different degrees can also suggest illusory differences between two bits of the same *koh*, and even the fragrance of the same piece of *koh* will come in waves, its intensity waxing and waning as the cup in which it nests is passed around the table.

After the test *koh* have been passed around the table, the *Koh* Master will say, *"Hon koh hajimemasu"* ("Now begins the real *koh*, the *koh* which have to be identified"). She puts her hand over a cup to check that the heat is sufficient, then opens a packet of paper to extract a sliver of *koh*—she doesn't know herself which *koh* it is—and carefully places it on the heated quartz square over the ashes. *"Hon koh ichi de gozaimasu,"* she intones ("Real *koh* number one") and passes the cup to the person on her right (just as in the tea ceremony), who lifts the cup with her right hand and turns it counterclockwise half a turn (just as in the tea ceremony), cups her left hand over the cup to focus the scent, and inhales softly three times.

There are different styles in listening to *koh*. Some people take their time between inhalations and close their eyes, a faint smile playing on their lips; some listen more matter-of-factly, nodding to themselves as if to say, "OK, message received." The cup proceeds around the table, everyone listening to the *koh* in turn and perhaps afterward making a discreet note so they can more easily formulate their responses after all the cups of *koh* have circulated.

By this time, the room is beginning to fill with mingled scents, which is delightfully confusing. (The classic *kohdo* setting is in a teahouse, where there is likely to be less of a problem of lingering scents. The members of the *kohdo* class will wear kimono to meet several times a year in a teahouse, most notably the beautiful teahouse on the grounds of Meiji Shrine, together with the members of other *kohdo* associations—the weekly classes are regarded only as practice sessions.)

As the last cup is passed back to the *Koh* Master, she announces, *"Hon koh taki owarimashita"* ("The *koh* fire is out") and everyone transcribes their answers on the slip of Japanese paper they have previously written their name on. You may need some help at this point because each of the test scents to which you must match the real scents has been given a name like "Snow" or "Wind" or "Flower." Then a tray is passed around to collect the answers. The Record Keeper writes everyone's answers on her large sheet of paper and ruthlessly ticks off the correct answers with vermilion ink.

Class members are generally very experienced in *kohdo* and several people will probably correctly match all the real scents with the test scents. Only at this point will you come to understand that *kohdo* requires very considerable skill.

The record of everyone's answers is passed around the table and the sensei may offer a gentle comment on the session's deceptive points. The large sheet of paper recording the answers is awarded to the person who has done best. There may be some unexpired *koh* left over, in which case lots are drawn for it, as people who appreciate *koh* like to enjoy it at home. Conversation turns to everyday matters, and as you leave the class you will smell the world outside with a heightened awareness.

To enter into the study of *kohdo*, you'll first have to introduce yourself to a teacher, who will invite you to join the practice sessions he or she oversees. There are two main schools of *kohdo*, and you'll have to align yourself with one or the other. The main difference in the schools seems to be how one holds one's arms as one partakes of the incense—modestly to the side of the body or in a more aggressive stance.

The school associated with the aristocracy is headed by Mr. Gyoun Sanjounishi, whose name card identifies him as the 22nd generation teacher of this school of *kohdo*. Sanjounishi-sensei, a kind and almost preternaturally modest man, is a relative of the dowager Empress of Japan. Sanjounishi-sensei holds practice sessions on the first and third Wednesday of every month in an elegant tatami room on the fifth floor of a building in the Ginza. Call **Koju**, a dealer in incense, at 3567-2104 to reserve a place at one of Sanjounishi-sensei's introductory sessions. It costs ¥5,000.

A teacher of the school founded by the samurai is Mariko Misuno, who can be contacted at her home in Tokyo at 3663-4880. Misuno-sensei holds introductory classes in Tokyo every Saturday.

Before making an inquiry of a teacher, though, you might like to get an idea of what you are getting yourself in for by taking a look at some of the equipment involved with *kohdo*. **Kyukyodo**, Ginza 5-7-4, which happens to be sitting on the most expensive real estate in Japan, has a second floor devoted to writing instruments and *kohdo* implements.

Just What Types of Wood Make Up *Koh*?

Ultimately, the attraction of this esoteric pastime is the koh *itself. The scent of these rare fragrant woods from Thailand, Vietnam, and Indonesia (remarkably,* koh *has never been available naturally in Japan) is delicious, as complex as the nose of a fine Bordeaux, but softer, less acrid. Compared to* koh, *perfume from the flask and ordinary stick incense seems crude stuff. In the end, people are drawn to* kohdo *because of its sensual pleasure, with the mind games a bonus for the wandering intellect.*

Koh is divided into six main types, rather like the appelations contrôlées *of wine, and each has many subdivisions. There is* kyara, *an elegant and sophisticated scent;* rakoku, *a somewhat less sophisticated scent that is more forward than* kyara; manaban, *a rustic, even boorish scent;* manaka, *a sexy, blatantly sensual scent;* sumontara, *a provocative, aggressive, argumentative scent; and* sasora, *perhaps the easiest scent to understand, which evokes cinnamon and wine in oak and which* kohdo *people describe as being austere, clerical, and uptight.*

Koh practitioners say that if you try to characterize koh *using the traditional terms used to describe taste—bitter, sour, sweet, hot, and salty —taste being closely related to smell, you will never understand* koh.

Koh people say that koh *transcends these matter-of-fact categories, that it is an experience in itself beyond words, and that entry into this quiet, extremely subtle world is marvelously relaxing.*

The Elegant Sport Called *Kyudo* 2

Kyudo is Japanese archery, a martial art born of war which has evolved into a graceful, contemplative ritual. Its intricate technique is enormously demanding: I know a man who has spent six years studying *kyudo*, practicing almost every day, who is quick to say he has only scratched the surface; I have a strong impression that this is not just *pro forma* Japanese modesty.

Kyudo is a good deal less in the public eye than the more flamboyantly aggressive martial arts like judo or kendo or karate (which is not native to these shores anyway) partly, one supposes, because it has absolutely no practical application—you are unlikely to have an arrow and a long Japanese bow handy when you next encounter a mugger—but also because the sport can only be viewed at a *kyudo dojo* (practice hall), of which there are only about a hundred in all of Tokyo, most of them hidden away down back alleys.

Nor are *kyudo dojo* places for the casual gawker. To be formally introduced to a *dojo* you must usually convince someone who is already associated with it that you are seriously interested in learning the sport, and this might well involve getting yourself fitted out with a complete practice uniform at a cost of about ¥15,000 just to demonstrate your sincerity. Only after you have managed to establish your good faith do you stand a chance of being introduced to the *dojo*'s teacher or *sensei*.

Then, if the sensei agrees to take you on, you can plan on spending several months practicing the basic sequence of forms with a faintly ridiculous training aid called the *gomuyumi* (the "rubber bow," a section of bamboo with a long rubber band attached to one end), bolstered only by occasional advice from any member of the *dojo* who shows interest in the faltering progress of a rank beginner, before— at long last—comes the grand day when the sensei hands you a real bow. From this point you still have a long way to go before you can expect to be allowed to stand on the firing line and shoot at an actual target.

So you can see that to be admitted to a *kyudo dojo* to witness a practice session is an extraordinary privilege. Fortunately, one particular *dojo* in Tokyo is genuinely accommodating to people who would like to witness a practice session with a view to deciding whether or not to take up the sport. The *dojo* of Toshima Ward is now the oldest in Tokyo, all of the city's *dojo* having been destroyed during the war and the sport banned by Occupation authorities.

Until he died in 1990 at the age of 80, the *dojo*'s teacher was Onuma-sensei. Onuma-sensei came from a family whose involvement with *kyudo* went back 15 generations. He himself had practiced *kyudo* for over 70 years and was one of the sport's acknowledged masters. It is because of Onuma-sensei that this *dojo* occupies a central position in the sport. *Kyudo* devotees come from all over the world to practice here.

The *dojo* currently has several teachers, but you would come across as pushy if you contacted one of them directly to ask permission to view a practice session. It would be better to make contact through the Physical Education Department (Taiiku-ka) of the Toshima Ward Office, whose telephone number is 3981-1111. They will arrange the necessary introductions.

If you do decide to attend a practice session, you should have more than a passing interest or curiosity about the sport. You should not drop into the *dojo* in the middle of a practice session, which can run to three hours, nor should you plan to leave before it is over. And during the practice session you should be as unobtrusive as possible so as not to disturb the concentration of the archers.

But the experience may change your life. You may find, after you have witnessed *kyudo* up close, that you would like to reserve a space in your own cluttered life for this elegant sport, which promises to teach more than just how to shoot a length of feathered bamboo through a circle of paper.

So, having made arrangements with the ward office, take the Yamanote Line to Otsuka and leave the station by the exit to the right as the train comes from Ikebukuro—the Minami Exit. The Toden trolley line, the city's last municipal trolley, clangs by in front of the station on its way to Waseda University at the end of the line, a Little Adventure for another day, perhaps. Follow the trolley tracks up the slope to the right. You are in a typical Tokyo neighborhood of bicycles, little bars teetering on the edge of respectability, and pachinko parlors on opposite sides of the road trying to drown each other out with blaring martial music and a patter of frantic announcements.

On the other side of the trolley tracks as you make your way up the hill are a couple of cheap restaurants specializing in *chuka ryori*, the Japanese version of everyday Chinese cooking. A bowl of *ramen* noodles for ¥450 at one of them will keep hunger in its place as you watch the practice.

Going up the hill you will also pass the shop of Yamaguchi, dealer in fine swords, whose dignified window display gives a clue to the venerated position of the martial arts in this country.

Peeking over the top of the hill you will see Ikebukuro's Sunshine Building, at 60 stories the tallest building in Japan, and at the top of the hill you will run into Kasuga-Dori, a major street (it has a name, after all). Look to the left and you will see the large yellow sign, surmounted by a round target, of Onuma-sensei's shop, **Asahi Kyugu** or "Asahi Archery Equipment." The address is 1931 Nishi Sugamo 2-chome (tel: 3971-2046).

You may want to stop in before going on to the *dojo*. Certainly a look at the shop's array of *kyudo* equipment will be instructive: the deerskin gloves with a bone-enforced thumb guard which, when you reach a certain rank, can be emblazoned with the family crest; the finely crafted bamboo arrows feathered with the tail plumage of a hawk or an eagle; and the laminated bamboo bows with a pull of up to 25 kilos or even more—to be held fully drawn without strain until the moment of release—which can cost up to ¥200,000.

The shop also carries Western archery equipment, which with its mass of pulleys, balances, and aiming devices is in sharp contrast to the mechanically very simple Japanese equipment. The shop sells for ¥500 a little book called *Japanese Archery: The Eight Rules*, written by Onuma-sensei when he was Professor of Archery at Gakushuin (Peers) University. The book, a nice keepsake, gives a hint of the complexity of the sport in its illustrations naming the 27 basic parts of the bow and the 11 basic parts of the arrow.

Leaving the shop, make your way back down Kasuga-Dori to the right past the Shell station, and turn left at the Nissan dealer at the corner. Go to the end of the road to the baseball field, turn right, and enter the building. (If you get lost, ask for **Toshima Sogo Taiiku-kan.**) You will see the entrance to the *dojo* on the right, with boxes for everyone's shoes. Enter, bow, and greet everyone with a cheery "*Konnichi wa!*"

Practice begins with everyone (including you) lining up in ranks on the *dojo*'s polished hardwood floor and, at a signal, bowing to the deity of the *dojo*. The sensei will then say *"Seiza!"* and everyone will sit in silence with their legs tucked under them for a few minutes (it will seem longer) in order to become calm.

Then the archers' names will be inscribed on the blackboard, bows unwrapped, and bow strings strung and waxed, and the first five archers will slip across the floor to their positions on the firing line. You will be offered a place in a little tatami area called the *kamiza* reserved for teachers and honored guests. From here you will be able to observe everything, to look right into the eyes of the archers, but you will not be able to observe the row of five paper targets 28 meters away. But it is not necessary for you to observe the targets; what will engage you is the stately ritual of firing performed so slowly it seems underwater. Performed confidently and in a relaxed manner, it is beautiful to watch, a dream-like dance.

After a while you will begin to spot the talent: that archer who takes his position solidly ("like a tree," the teacher will insist), whose left hand locks the bow into position seemingly without effort, whose progression through the eight distinct forms is one fluid movement, to the point where the bow is fully drawn, the arrow tight against the cheek, wait-wait-wait, then the snap of release.

It is very apparent who is in control and who is still awash. Those in control show no emotion, even after the release, and the muscles in their neck are always relaxed, even when the bow is fully drawn.

No one talks. The only sound is the creak of deerskin gloves as the bows are drawn and the swoosh of the release. Occasionally the teacher will say something like, "Keep your body straight!" or "Hold it. Hold it. Hooold it!" or "Unmmma *TSAK!*" (to indicate the feeling one should get from a good release), and the student will murmur an acknowledgement. This is teaching by suggestion, by the merest touch to an elbow a little too far forward. The goal is grace under pressure—the bow is sometimes held fully drawn for ten seconds or more—and a quiet humility.

By the end of the practice session every student will have been to the firing line five times and shot ten arrows altogether, hardly rapid fire. The score is kept on the blackboard, but there is absolutely no sense of competition. Indeed, *kyudo* people are apt to speak of some-one who can consistently hit the target as though he were good at a trivial trick, like shuffling a deck of cards.

After practice, everyone gathers on tatami mats around a low table for tea and sweet cakes and it is then you realize that the participants in this intensively choreographed discipline, who have seemed so pas-sionately detached from the world while they were shooting, are, in fact, just ordinary people after all.

Zazen: **A Lesson in Sitting Quietly** 3

Zen is training to be at every instant sharply aware of the heartbeat of the universe while at the same time remaining relaxed and calm—sort of the consciousness of a happy baby seems to be the ideal. You do this by learning how to empty your mind of everyday preoccupations like itches, sexual throbbing, anxiety about money, and that reoccur-ring daydream about driving a red Ferrari along the Corniche with an admirer at your side.

Adherents to zen say the non-zen mind chases after ideas like a monkey chases after peanuts. Zen is a tough, tough physical and mental discipline with a literature that celebrates embracing the Cosmic Absurd and planting a great wet kiss on its cheek. Zen is about sitting quietly. Zen is about nothing at all.

Every Monday evening, the zen temple of **Chokoku-ji** in Nishi Azabu offers an opportunity for the curious to experience something of the discipline of zen. Chokoku-ji's is an unstressful initiation: if you seriously petitioned a zen temple to accept you as a monk, you could be kept waiting on the doorstep of the temple in the snow for three days, as a preliminary test of your sincerity.

Chokoku-ji, founded in 1598, is the Tokyo branch of Eihei-ji, the great zen temple in Fukui Prefecture on the Japan Sea, an astonishing place well worth a visit. (The gravel path to the entrance of Eihei-ji is lined with cedars planted by the temple's third patriarch. It is numbing to walk down a path lined with trees a hundred feet tall and 600 years old.)

The Tokyo temple consists of three main buildings: the *Kannon-do* just inside the gate, where anyone can pop in for a quick obeisance to the four-story-high wooden statue of Kannon, the Buddhist goddess of mercy, or just sit for a while on one of the benches (donated by Fuji Film) along the back wall and inhale the incense; the main building or Hon-do, which is built entirely of Japanese cypress—the only such building in the city; and the Zen-do, the meditation hall, where you will spend the largest part of the evening.

Present yourself around 6:45 p.m. at the *uketsuke*, the reception area. Take off your shoes and stow them in the rack in the *genkan*, the entrance area. Kneel on a cushion before the little writing desk and inscribe your name and address in the temple's book, then slip a ¥100 coin into the offertory box, which is the only cost of this Little Adventure.

One of the monks will lead you down a dim corridor to a tatami room where you can divest yourself of your socks and your watch and any piece of clothing, such as a tie, that binds. This tatami room has something of the atmosphere of a locker room before an athletic event. The old hands are getting into their various zen-style meditation outfits and warming up with stretching exercises. Some sit immobile looking out of the window at a leafy scene—apparently as content as a bug.

As a neophyte, you will be led back to the reception area to a kind of dentist's waiting room (stuffed chairs, a rack of newspapers) to wait with the evening's dozen or so other neophytes for a monk to lead you all to the Hon-do for instruction on how to sit and how to move.

The Hon-do is a very large tatami room whose roof is supported by carved beams of great nobility. You line up in front of a rank of black, round cushions and listen while a monk explains with great authority how to walk, how to hold your hands as you walk, how to do *"gassho"* to greet another person, the proper way to care for and sit on your cushion and an alternative way for those who aren't quite prepared to sit in the classic *zazen* position of right ankle on left thigh, left ankle on right thigh, back absolutely straight, hands composed in the prescribed fashion, eyes half-closed, breathing regularly with tip of the tongue resting light on the front of the roof of the mouth.

It's all in Japanese, of course, but it's all clear enough. At ten minutes before eight, instruction is over and you are excused to go to the bathroom (you should bow to the bathroom shrine before using the facilities) and otherwise prepare to enter the meditation hall.

At precisely 8 p.m. you will be summoned into the Zen-do. The experienced practitioners are already there in their places on raised tatami mats facing the wall. The neophytes file in, slip on slippers, are given a little sutra booklet—a sort of Buddhist psalter (yours will be written in Roman letters). The monks will show you how to divest yourself of your slippers, *gassho* to the person across the aisle, and in a prescribed movement flip yourself onto your cushion and turn to face the wall.

And there you are, alone with yourself. Thoughts buzz around like mosquitoes and you are more uncomfortable than you have ever been in your life. Your knees are on fire. But the room of 60 people is absolutely quiet and as far as you can tell no one has shifted position so much as a millimeter. Gradually you don't feel your knees any more and your thoughts become fuzzy, drifting, lazy.

You snap back when from the center of the dimly lit room someone begins to speak. It is the teacher, and he talks softly about Great Things with easy pauses between sentences.

Then comes the chanting of the sutra. It is dull and monotonous and goes on and on, but there is harmony to it. Then a thumping of the huge drum in the corner and the rhythmic clatter of blocks of wood being beaten together, and it is over. You have been sitting for 40 minutes, and are slightly stunned by the ritual of it all.

Retreat to the tatami room to reclaim your gear (your watch will say 9 o'clock), and to the entrance to retrieve your shoes, then out into the night. Ha! The world is still here!

If you are in the mood for a bite to eat, 20 meters down the street, across from the Fuji Building, is a fine little Indian restaurant called **Bindi** which specializes in home-style cooking.

Chokoku-ji (tel: 3400-5232) is at 21-34 Nishi Azabu 2-chome, just around the corner from the Fuji Building, which is a landmark in this part of town. It's a ten-minute walk from the Omotesando subway exit B-1.

4 Two Gardens

Here is a way to wile away a lazy afternoon any season of the year. First a light lunch of *soba* (buckwheat noodles) at a famous old Tokyo noodle shop, then a stroll through two adjacent parks. One the landscaped, manicured grounds of the residence of a prince, with lawns like a Cambridge college; the other a national nature conservancy, a 50-acre piece of land that has been left just as it was before there was a city here, the last existing natural part of the Musashi Plain, with great mossy trees 500 years old—there's nothing like it in any city anywhere in the world.

That it could exist in hard-charging Tokyo, a city normally intent on excavation, is nothing short of miraculous.

Exit Meguro Station onto Meguro Dori and turn left. Eighty me ters down the street you will see a sign:

Shizenkyoikuen   470m

Teien Art Museum   420m

which is where you are going. On the next corner, you will see another sign announcing the presence of a Chinese restaurant called Han, which, however, is not where you are going.

Turn left here and go 50 meters to a plain, worn wooden house on the left hand side of the street. This is the *soba* shop called **Issa-an**, celebrated for its handmade noodles and its utter lack of pretension, which is where I suggest lunch. (Note, though, that Issa-an is not open Wednesdays.) Divest yourself of your shoes in the little entrance way. A waitress in kerchief and jeans will show you to one of the low tables in one of the tatami-matted rooms, then she will kneel to solicit your order, which might be, for example:

Seiro (¥730)—an order of plain noodles, or

Nishoku (¥1,000)—two different kinds of plain noodles, or

Sanshoku (¥1,580)—three different kinds of plain noodles, or (if you are in an extravagant mood)

Yuzukiri (¥1,220)—*soba* noodles flavored with the juice of the *yuzu*, a delicate Japanese citrus fruit.

A ¥420 order of pickles would add crunch. This is the way a *soba* connoisseur orders.

Take a look at the kitchen out back before you leave. There is a huge pot of boiling water, a board on which to cut the noodles, racks of the bowls and a single jolly chef. Couldn't be simpler. The little cabinet in the entrance way displays things customers satiated to forgetfulness have left behind: a key chain, a tortoiseshell shoe horn, an earring, a tiny pine cone. They will probably be here in this cabinet when you come back.

Head down the road now, to the **Teien Art Museum**. It costs ¥100 to enter the garden with an extra charge, the amount depending on what is on exhibit, to enter the museum itself. The museum used to be the private house of Prince Asaka, the eighth son of Prince Kuni. He married Princess Nobuko, the eighth daughter of Emperor Meiji. The prince studied in Paris, where he became enamored of Art Deco, and he commissioned Henri Rapin, a French architect in great vogue at the time, to design this house for him and his bride. The house was completed in 1933 and is far and away Tokyo's best example of the genre, with wonderful doors and lighting fixtures and banks of heroic Lalique glass.

Unfortunately, the house was turned into a museum with a heavy hand. It should be completely open to the public, its doors and windows thrown open to the garden, period furniture, and bibelots put on display, concerts of Stravinsky and Satie held every weekend in the Great Hall and characterful restaurants installed in each of the house's two dining halls. Perhaps someday....

But the prince's garden is very pleasant, although it is closed on the second and fourth Wednesday of the month, unless one of those days is a national holiday, in which case it will be closed the next day—except if there is a full moon (just kidding). Here we have a secluded teahouse, a pond with lolling carp, a rolling landscape with groves of trees, comfortable wooden benches under the trees, and tables and chairs scattered about—a singular rarity for Tokyo—on the grass. Families come to spread a picnic and watch their children frolic in disbelief that such a place could exist except in fairy tales.

Prince Asaka's garden is for its fans Tokyo's most congenial public park, for indulging in *dolce far niente*, for putting one's face up to the sun, for sitting and reading a slow-moving novel, or for catching up on one's more frivolous correspondence. Too many of Tokyo's parks are either so crowded you cannot linger, or so restrictive you can only shuffle along a narrow, roped-off path, so the good prince has bestowed on us a benefaction.

But do not linger here past 3 p.m. or you will not be permitted to enter **Shizenkyoikuen**, the National Science Museum's Institute for

Nature Study, which is right next door. (Linger all you like on Mondays, though, as on this day Shizenkyoikuen is closed.)

Depending on your mood, Shizenkyoikuen will probably be the high point of the afternoon. It costs ¥210 to enter, which buys you a ribbon to pin on. Because there are only 300 ribbons and because you have to return your ribbon when you leave, the number of people allowed in at any one time is limited, praise be. This is a serious, Japanese-type place and sometimes there are lectures. There may be a notice: "Today's research theme is spiders."

Inside, with so much greenery, the air is pure. Along the walk, plants have been cultivated for delectation in their variety: *Hitorishizuka* ("Alone and quiet"), *Futarishizuka* ("Two quiet together"), *Yaburegasa* ("Crumpled hat"), *Jamohige* ("Snake's moustache"). Many of these species could not be allowed in a cultivated garden, as they are mere, but marvelous, weeds.

There are about 8,000 trees in here, of all sorts, even palm trees. Every eight years a select band of students of horticulture from Tokyo's universities conduct a tree census, registering the height and girth of every tree in a series of large notebooks. (Unbridled nature is an excellent concept, a fine subject for study.)

Photographers in safari dress come with tripods and huge lenses to photograph the curve of pampas grass against the sky. The only sound is the crunch of gravel on the path and the call of birds. Here raw nature seems somnolent, not tooth and nail. Leaves fall thick on the ground. Parasitic vines entwine. Mushrooms grow on the sign posts. In a murky pond, turtles lounge on a log. A wooden bridge winds through the lily pads and a huge carp patrols like a drowsy submarine.

One section is roped off, because a tree is about to fall. When it does, it will be left as it falls. A huge 300-year-old pine, of a species called *kuramatsu* which has no branches, snakes into the sky. Old plants wither, new ones green, but a stand of *konara*, good wood for charcoal, grows so thick that young trees of its species can get no sun, and so in a hundred years the pines, whose young require less sun, will take over.

As we leave, we resolve to come back the next season, when it will all be different.

5   A Walk Through Old Tokyo

In Japanese terms, Tokyo isn't an old city at all. It's only about as old as Boston. And because twice in this century it has been all but obliterated—once by the Great Kanto Earthquake in 1923 and once by the firebombing of 1945 which spared only one building in ten—and also because a hefty percentage of the people who live in the city were not born here, there are few sections of Tokyo that evoke in anyone a nostalgia for things past.

Any Tokyoite will tell you, however, that the adjoining neighborhoods of Sendagi, Nezu and Yanaka near Ueno are the best places to go to get a sense of how things used to be, and it is to this part of the city that young scholars from Stanford and the Sorbonne come to rent old houses with rock gardens while they put the finishing touches on their dissertations on Kafu the Scribbler or the Staging of the Noh Drama.

They find here the essential coziness of the old style of Japanese urban living, with a lively street life, public baths that serve as neighborhood social clubs and shopkeepers who make a habit of setting aside something for their best customers, which means anybody who has ever dropped by twice. Sendagi, Nezu, and Yanaka make up the core of *shitamachi* Tokyo (the old "downtown").

This walk through the area can take as long as seven hours, depending on how good you are at lingering and on how contemplative a mood you are in. Even if you take me up on most of my recommendations, the day should cost no more than ¥5,000. Note that if you take the walk on a Monday or Friday, you won't be able to get into the Asakura Choso Museum, which is closed on those days. This would be a great pity.

Go to Sendagi Station on the Chiyoda Line. If you are coming from the direction of Hibiya, as you probably will be, sit near the front of the train so when you get off you'll be near the Dokanyama

ADVENTURE 5

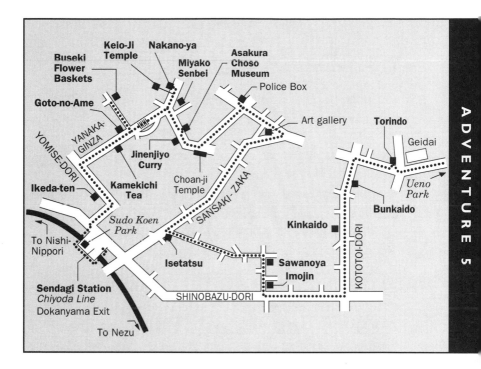

Exit, by which you should leave the station. This will put you on Shinobazu-dori, the area's main street. Turn right on Shinobazu-dori, then immediately turn right again into a narrow alley, at the end of which is

1. **Sudo Koen Park**. Tokyo has more than 7,000 parks, ranging from the rolling Shinjuku-gyoen to pocket parks just big enough for a single bench. Sudo Koen is a medium-size park taken absolutely for granted by the people of the neighborhood who come here to eat lunch, watch the children play, and doze off. It is a very Tokyo sort of park, with its landscaping all out of scale with the size of the park (it tries hard to make you think it is bigger than it is), its dusty pool of carp, and its vermilion Shinto shrine on a little island.

Cross the red bridge and walk around the shrine past the waterfall out to the right. Leave the park and take the alley in front of you back out to Shinobazu-Dori.

Turn left on Shinobazu-Dori and cross it at the next traffic signal, 20 meters away. Five years ago, none of these tall, totally undistinguished buildings you see along Shinobazu-Dori were here. Residents feel their way of life threatened.

Go down the street going off from Shinobazu-Dori at the traffic signal, leaving the hulking presence of the NTT Building on your right. At the end of this short street, turn left onto "Yomise Dori," so written in *kana* over the Buck Rogers-style arch spanning this street of typical old downtown shops.

There's a rice merchant (ten kilos for ¥6,500—so expensive because the rice farmers are heavily subsidized and the outlets strictly controlled), a shop selling all manner of footgear from plastic sandals to wooden *geta*, a tofu maker, a saké shop, and on the left

2. **Ikeda-ten**, the *kamaboko* (fish cake) maker, under a blue awning. A quick Tokyo snack here, maybe? Ask for *ba-ru* and you will get for ¥100 five balls of deep-fried squid tentacles and chopped onion, perfect for munching on while walking, a little pleasure not yet full sanctioned by Japanese etiquette but which here in *shitamachi* is perfectly O.K.

Stroll on by the vegetable store with everything laid out precisely and the *konnyaku* maker with his great wooden and plastic mixing tubs. (Kenkyusha's Japanese-English Dictionary identifies *konnyaku* as "a paste made from the starch of devil's tongue," which only serves to underline the essentiality of experience over mere description.)

Even at the risk of the shopkeeper's not being able to move around in his tiny shop, everything is laid out for the customer to see and before any purchase can be made, it is necessary to pass the time of day. There is a bond here between merchant and customer which may well go back generations on each side.

On your right at the corner you'll come to a shop called Toho which sells *bento* lunch boxes. Next to it is a rather self-conscious archway labeled "Yanaka Ginza" in *kana*. Turn right through this arch onto a tiled road, very fancy, as befits the neighborhood's main shopping street.

Along Yanaka Ginza you will also find a wondrous profusion of shops, most with their goods for sale and their carefully tended pots of flowers and greenery spilling out into the street: a florist; a saké merchant; a store selling underwear; a toy shop; a barbershop, whose customers are submitted to an almost clinical concern (a Little Adventure for another day is a visit to a Japanese barber); a large fish store with an amazing variety of sea creatures laid out on ice, illuminated at dusk by lights as if jewelry. Then on the same side of the street you will come to the wonderful shop called

3. **Kamekichi Tea Merchants**. Go in, all the way to the back, to the finely tooled brass mural of cranes which decorates the doors of the shop's refrigerated storeroom. In the back of the shop there is a lovely garden off to the left, a little secret that everyone in the neighborhood knows about and now you do, too. Everyone also knows that every visitor is without fail offered a cup of tea; you can sip yours while inspecting the implements for sale and the many different kinds of tea shipped to the shop from Shizuoka, Saitama, and Kyushu in wooden chests.

The most expensive tea is *Tenshi*, 100 grams for ¥3,000, but ordinary *ocha* for daily drinks (Japanese when they first go abroad say the first thing they miss is *ocha*) is ¥300 for 100 grams. If the weather is fine the shop might put out in the street its battered old roasting machine which, as it turns the tea leaves over, produces a lovely, beckoning scent.

On the left just at the end of Yanaka Ginza, past the hardware store, the chicken-parts store, the gardening-supplies store, the stationery store and the kimono store which has found out that in order to survive it must also sell fur coats, just as the tiles give way to ordinary paving, you will find

4. **Goto-no-Ame** ("Goto's Candies"), an old-fashioned sweet shop which recently sold out to Monteyamazaki, a chain. As you can surmise from the sound of the ancient machinery grinding away out back, the shop still makes ten kinds of candy of its own. I am partial to the delicately sweetened hard candies called *Tankiri* at ¥250 a packet,

while a lady I know prefers the *Shoga Ame* (same price) which is made of ginger.

At this point you might want to consider a quick detour. Running off the end of Yanaka Ginza to the left is a street, and 50 meters down you will come across

5. **Buseki Flower Basket Shop**. Here the friendly Buseki-san, who dresses in comfortable Edo-style home wear, and his son, who favors Ralph Lauren sweatshirts, make the most exquisite baskets and vases out of well-smoked bamboo 100 years old, which they have procured from under the thatched roofs of country cottages.

You will be most graciously received, probably offered tea, and invited to inspect some of the shop's work, like the beautiful vase just put on reserve by the Portuguese Ambassador or the little tray of woven bamboo for ¥500, which just might suit you—who knows?

Now back to Yanaka Ginza, to turn left to go up the stairs. On the left as you go up the hill you will pass one temple, then come to another. This is

6. **Keio-ji**, a fine neighborhood temple suffused with greenery. The temple's cemetery runs along the left, and to the right is a little building which has a long bench made of a single piece of wood running along under the eaves—a good place to sit down and try one of Goto's candies, if you bought some.

The most remarkable thing about this temple is the intricate system of copper pipes for draining water from the roof of the temple into the great stone cauldrons on either side of the stairs. This Rube Goldberg contraption has a purpose: the system provides water to fight a fire.

What's that low rumble from the building next door? Well, the building next door houses

7. **Nakano-ya**, manufacturers and purveyors of *tsukudani*, a sort of Japanese chutney made by marinating various things in a mixture of soy sauce, rice vinegar, and saké to preserve them—there were no refrigerators in the days when everybody ate *tsukudani* every day—to be spread over the top of a bowl of rice and eaten while drinking *ocha*.

This is real Tokyo provender—you won't find *tsukudani* in a restaurant. Most *tsukudani* costs ¥250 for 100 grams, but for a real *tsukudani*-connoisseur's treat you might like to try *unagi yamato ni* (marinated eel), 100 grams of which go for ¥1,400. This is not street-eating food, though.

Cross the street in front of the temple and continue on down the street that bears off from the main street in the same direction. (You'll see a marble-monument store on the corner.) There is a little alleyway off to the left, then a flower shop, then a Chinese restaurant, and then a covered arcade, which you should enter. A few meters in on the left you will discover

8. **Miyako Senbei**, an old shop selling rice crackers made here. Notice the four old hand blown glass globes in which the *senbei* are kept. Their best seller is a packet of *goma* (sesame seed) *senbei* for ¥200.

Now go back down the arcade to turn left again on the street, the direction you were going in when you entered. This street of old shops includes on the right a maker of copper kitchen tools, who displays his wares and other *objets* he thinks amusing in a little vitrine he has built into his shop and just after it, on the left, is what appears to be a huge black bunker with a kneeling figure of bronze perched on the roof as if daring someone to ask him to jump. From the outside, the place certainly looks forbidding, but inside is the high point of this Little Adventure. It's the

9. **Asakura Choso Museum** (¥300 entrance fee. Closed Mondays and Fridays, December 29 to January 3, and any day after a national holiday). It really isn't a museum in the ordinary sense. It's the atelier, house, and magnificent rock and water garden of Fumio Asakura, a sculptor, scholar, and contemplator of the meaning of life who died in 1954, at the age of 82. He designed the house and garden himself and it took six years to complete because the builders had never seen plans for anything like it before.

The garden settles everyone down as soon as they see it, a place of great tranquility on a wonderfully intimate scale. It is designed so that some plant is always in bloom, something always showing some color. The huge carp move slowly in the two-meter-deep pond. Underneath a rock as smooth and voluptuous as a Maillol sculpture—the rock nicknamed *okame ishi*—there is a place hollowed out for the carp.

In winter, you can warm yourself next to a pit of glowing charcoal set into the floor of a little room overlooking the pond for as long as you like. When it snows here, it is lovely. In the summer, the shoji are removed and the rooms are open to the garden.

You may want to wander further, to the second floor, to the third, to the roof. You may be offered a cup of tea in the atelier before you go. It is a shame to rush on, but as we all get caught up in one thing or another and might never have a chance to see more, perhaps we'd better go.

Exit this miraculous place and turn left, continuing down the same road. Almost immediately on your right, you will come across

10. **Jinenjiyo Curry Shop**, which grows all its own herbs and which would be a fine place for lunch.

There is a temple every 50 meters, it seems. Nothing higher than two stories here, because when this part of town was built, people were very conscious of the wrath of the Earthquake God. More little alleys crammed with potted plants and bicycles.

After a few hundred meters, you will come on the right to Choan-ji Temple, so marked with a rakish sign in English. Turn left here. We are going to walk through Yanaka Bochi—Yanaka Cemetery.

Turn right at the police box and continue along a tree-lined road where you will find a number of flower shops patronized by people paying a visit to the family grave who want to leave some flowers and perhaps something the deceased particularly enjoyed, such as a bottle of saké or a bar of chocolate.

At the little art gallery, bear right under the *icho* trees, whose leaf is heart-shaped, a common Tokyo design motif. The street curves around to the left and the sidewalk is confidently paved. Now we will visit, if you like, a series of craft shops. We go down the hill called Sansaki-zaka—*saka* or *zaka* means "slope." Every single shop has its pots of flowers or vines out front, as a talisman to keep urbanity at bay. Again, there seems to be a temple every 50 meters. At the bottom of Sansaki-zaka, on the left-hand side of the street, you'll come across

11. **Isetatsu Decorated Papers**. Here they carve out of wooden blocks the patterns which adorn their papers. There is a great variety, some of the blocks having been carved in the era of Emperor Meiji. The more sophisticated (and expensive) papers are on the second floor. A print from a classic block can cost ¥7,000 or more.

At Isetatsu, turn left off Sansaki-zaka and go down a very ordinary downtown street, neither modern nor traditional but caught, as is most of the city, somewhere between. At the Kodak sign follow the road as it curves around to the left.

Take the first right at Sawanoya, an inexpensive (¥4,600 a night) Japanese-style hotel. Down this street on the left-hand side at the second corner you will come across

12. **Imojin**, an old-fashioned ice-cream shop. It couldn't be plainer, a lovely old place, with what must be the world's first take-out window on the side. This is not fancy ice cream of many flavors, but honest, unadulterated stuff just like the ice cream families must have made themselves before it was easy to buy ice cream in a store. It is made on the premises, of course.

If you ask for *abekku*, you will be served a dish with a scoop of vanilla and a scoop of *azuki*-bean ice cream for ¥200. *Abekku* is the French *avec*, ice cream for two, you and your date.

As you exit the shop turn left, then left again on Shinobazu-Dori. (Although it's another distraction, if you cross Shinobazu-Dori here the street will take you right to Nezu Jinja shrine, the progenitor of all the dozens of shrines you have seen today.) Go three traffic lights to Kototoi-Dori, so labeled, and turn left onto it. After 100 meters the street will begin to rise. This is Zenkoji-zaka. Almost at the top of the slope on the left-hand side of the street will be

13. **Kinkaido**, a shop which sells color. Japanese-style paintings, called *nihonga*, do not use oils. The colors are from minerals, plants, and insects which are glued to a board or canvas. This shop is ablaze

with colors, all in glass vials in wooden racks. They make the eyes swim. Art students from nearby Tokyo University of the Arts come here or to the competing shop across the street to buy their materials.

Turn left as you exit the shop and continue on up Kototoi-Dori. On the right-hand side of the street, just after the Konica sign, you will find

14. **Bunkaido**. Mr. Tanabe, the shopkeeper, has made brushes for Miró and Picasso. He has made a brush so large it takes three men to hold it and guide it through a fierce, swooping *kanji*. You could buy one of Mr. Tanabe's brushes for ¥1,700 if you like, or maybe a *mizuire*, a tiny vessel to keep water for mixing ink, for ¥300 to ¥1,300.

Back on Kototoi-Dori on the right hand side of the road, and on through the traffic signal. At the second light by the sushi shop, turn right into an alley. (In case you are wondering, that edifice diagonally across from this corner is a replica of an old saké shop.) Past Pepe le Moko, a little French restaurant of no particular distinction. At the end of this alley on the left you will find

15. **Torindo**, a perfect place for a cup of tea if you can make it before 5 p.m. when they close. A lovely little shop. Just say *"Ocha kudasai,"* and maybe point out one of the *wagashi* cakes to go with it. The tea will cost ¥450 and the cake maybe ¥150.

Now let's go home. To return to more familiar surroundings, cross the street. Geidai (Tokyo University of the Arts) will be on your left as you walk toward Ueno Park. At the beginning of the next block you will come across the (now closed) Dobutsuen Hakubutsukan Station of the Keisei subway line, which looks like a sullen Greek temple.

Or you can just keep walking down the street to the Tokyo National Museum on your left, at which you should cross the street to enter Ueno Park. In the park, go around the pool lined with benches, turn left at the plaza at the end of the pool and, with the National Museum of Western Art on your left and the Le Corbusier-designed Tokyo Metropolitan Festival Hall (Tokyo Bunka Kaikan) on your right, cross the street to Ueno Station.

Minka-en: Magnificent Old Farmhouses   6

Some people dream of living in a sleek penthouse ringed by a wide terrace from which they could look out on a twinkling city every evening. Others imagine that they could find contentment in a small Queen Anne country house of perfect proportions. Still others would like nothing better than to live out their days in a simple Polynesian hideaway set back from a silken beach.

If I had my choice, I would make my home in an old Japanese farmhouse.

This is not a personal quirk. Many people, Japanese as well as foreigners, have been struck by the quiet harmonies of traditional Japanese rural architecture. Some have gone so far as to buy one of the magnificent old farmhouses called *minka* and have it disassembled and reconstructed on their plot of land in Kamakura or Kauai or Rio. City peoples' fantasies about living this way are in fact now so commonplace that if you should approach a real estate agent in rural Japan and tell him that you are looking for a house, he will begin drawing up a list of abandoned *minka* for you to inspect.

Minka of classic design in reasonably good condition are difficult to come across, however. They have been recognized as the treasures they are: the most beautiful dwellings ever produced by a rustic agrarian society. Assuming you could find one, it might well cost as much as you would pay for a modern house, and if you wanted to move your *minka* (which is entirely feasible as these old farmhouses were constructed without nails), you would need to hire a crew of expert Japanese carpenters as well as a heavy crane, because a *minka*'s structural beams are massive, weighing a ton. These houses were built as Stonehenge was built, to last forever.

Although you might not be in a position just at the moment to think seriously about buying your own *minka*, you can prepare yourself for that eventuality by inspecting a collection of 20 superb examples of *minka* gathered from all over Japan—most of them solemnly designated "Important Cultural Properties" by the Japanese government—in a tranquil, garden-like setting just a half hour from Shinjuku. It makes for a pleasant half-day outing and offers the best possible insight into the genius of Japan's traditional architecture.

At Shinjuku Station, buy a ¥200 ticket for Mukogaoka-yuen on the Odakyu Line. Leave Mukogaoka-yuen by the South Exit. You'll see a map posted showing how to get to **Nihon Minka-en**. It's about a 20-minute walk straight through town out into the surrounding hills. just follow the monorail tracks until they bear off to the left. You keep going straight. It's ¥300 to enter.

At the top of a short slope you encounter the first *minka*, a 150-year-old inn with a built-in stable. Walk right in. It is cool and dark inside, as open as a forum. The inn of Suzuki could put up perhaps 20 guests and their horses. Here, as in all houses in Minka-en, a plaque explains in Japanese and English the provenance of the structure, and you can inspect a faded photograph showing it in its original setting.

Next is the house of Ioka, the dwelling of a merchant who sold lamp oil and incense in Nara 260 years ago. As you leave Ioka's house, you will hear the muffled thumping of the 120-year-old mill and the groan of a water wheel.

Then the house of Sasaki, who was chief of his village in Nagano. This is perhaps the most beautiful *minka* of them all, with an utterly unadorned facade 25 meters across and delicate beams and pillars. The house is open to nature, and off to one side is a sophisticated little garden.

The route from house to house is well-marked. You wind along the path through the woods, and when you emerge into a clearing there will be a *minka* like Emukai's 250-year-old *gassho zukuri*-style house from Toyama Prefecture, with its great cathedral-like roof pitched very steeply in order to prevent snow from accumulating, or the elegant house of Yamada with its brass door fittings, tatami edged with brocade, and a thatched roof two feet thick which serves to keep the house warm in winter and cool in summer.

Yamashita's house is majestic, with a roof soaring as high as a modern four- or five-story building. Why not stop here for lunch? A bowl of *sansai soba* (noodles with various mountain ferns) is ¥600. In the cold weather you sit on cushions around a wood fire set into the middle of the floor, just as did the Yamashitas.

The *minka* are arranged as if in a mountain village. A fine balance is struck between the need to protect and preserve the houses and the desirability of maintaining the illusion they remain in their original setting.

There is a storehouse from Okinawa, built like a little temple, and the house of Hirose, with thick walls and small windows and straw mats strewn around like area rugs, and a tiny altar tucked away in the eaves. (*Minka*, as the houses of the peasantry, were not allowed to have *tokonoma* in which to hang scrolls, and decoration for decoration's sake is virtually non-existent.)

The houses, which are pervaded by the lingering aroma of wood smoke, are held together by prodigies of tying—split bamboo and hempen ropes. A small room in a *minka* is 16 mats, twice the size of a large room in a posh modern Tokyo apartment. But *minka* had to be large: some of them sheltered extended families of 50.

Up a steep path to an antique Kabuki theater brought here from a fishing village in Mie Prefecture, then down to a valley containing a cluster of houses from the Tohoku area and a tiny boatman's hut (circa 1939), evocative of Thoreau's hut on Walden Pond. You think: yes, I could live like this. When you leave by the rear exit of Minka-en, keep bearing left past the fountain, past the planetarium, and you will come out where you entered.

Minka-en is closed Mondays and some holidays. Call 044-922-2181 to check.

7 Tea in the Garden of a Kamakura Temple

Kamakura, a town of some 150,000 souls, is beautifully situated in the hills which run down to Sagami Bay. Because it's less than an hour from Tokyo Station on the blue train of the Yokosuka Line and because of its history (it was Japan's administrative capital for 250 years) and tranquil beauty (it has over 80 shrines and temples), it is a favored place of residence of artists, writers, academics, and people who want to be close to Tokyo but not *too* close. On a weekday in the off-season Kamakura has an elegiac feeling to it, like Kyoto, but on a sunny Saturday or Sunday in the summer the place turns into a madhouse seaside resort, its streets filled with people consulting guidebooks and shepherding children with balloons. Schedule your visit with this in mind.

When the train pulls into Kita (North) Kamakura you will sense a change from the drab industrial landscape through which you have just traveled. Here there are rocks and pools and little off-hand gardens. At Kamakura Station, the next stop, take the East Exit. Do the people who live in Kamakura speak more softly? They seem more relaxed, certainly.

One of the great set pieces of Kamakura is the walk up Wakamiya Oji-Dori to the great shrine called Tsurugaoka Hachimangu. The shrine was founded in 1063 and from its heights there is a commanding view of the city. Buy a fortune for ¥100 from a temple maiden and if you don't like it, tie it neatly on a tree and it won't count. It's roughly a two-kilometer walk, most of it along a busy public highway to Hokoku-ji where we will take tea. The Nameri River, off to your right, is two feet deep at most and is home to carp and ducks.

As soon as you turn off the highway onto the road to Hokoku-ji, it becomes still. Within a two-kilometer radius of this spot there are seven temples. The stones in the gurgling stream feeding into Namerikawa are mossy and cool.

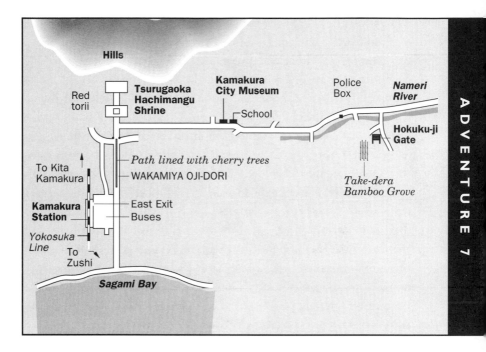

Enter Hokoku-ji's gate and go up the worn stone steps to Take-dera, the name of the bamboo grove on the grounds of the temple. Slip a ¥100 coin into the wooden turnstile to gain admission. The grove consists of several hundred magnificent bamboo shooting up 30 meters or so, a dreamy place. With the bamboo curving in at the top, it's like a green cathedral. Yasunari Kawabata, Japan's Nobel Prize-winning novelist and hometown boy, called this place Yama-no-oto, "The Sound of Mountains," because it reminded him of a place where nothing can be heard but the rustling of leaves.

Take-dera's tea pavilion is situated so it looks out onto the grove and garden. A bowl of thick *matcha* tea, the tea of the tea ceremony, is ¥300. It is prepared for you with an absent-minded flip of a bamboo whisk—a far cry from the complex ritual of an actual tea ceremony, but we're all friends here. Many of the people who make their way to Take-dera are carrying cameras and are on a kind of pilgrimage.

First eat the two *okashi* sweet cakes that come with your bowl of tea. They will prime your taste buds for the faintly bitter taste of the tea. The formal ritual of a proper tea ceremony, according to one authority, requires 331 separate points to be observed. We can at least observe one: the tea should be drunk in three and a half sips with a sound made at the end like sucking up the last of a milkshake with a straw. At Take-dera, ceremony is minimal. Stay as long as you like....

But the real reason to come to Kamakura, the real Little Adventure, is the chance to explore the back roads going up into the hills. Kamakura is on a perfect scale to explore by foot. There are signposts everywhere to the nearest temples, some of which are within a hundred meters of each other. Most are now uninhabited and to visit them is like chancing on a ghostly place. As you go up into the hills on narrow winding streets and rural lanes, you come across thick hedgerows, unexpected outbursts of flowers, quiet shops, ancient bridges on the edge of decay, gates hiding secluded houses, well-trimmed pine trees, and crusty stone lions encroached by ferns. I leave it to you to find your own temple. No need to hurry; the town becomes softer as the sun sets and the lanterns begin to flicker.

8 The Mingei-kan and the Marquis' Garden

The folk art of pre-industrial Japan—the bowls and boxes and kettles and pickle jars made for everyday use—is amazing stuff. In *mingei* ("the people's art") you can catch a glimpse of the same inspired simplicity that characterizes the furniture of the American Shakers. There is a genius to it.

Some people think the **Mingei-kan**, a museum devoted to these everyday artifacts, is the most revelatory of Tokyo's several hundred museums. It is true, at any rate, that an hour or two in this graceful

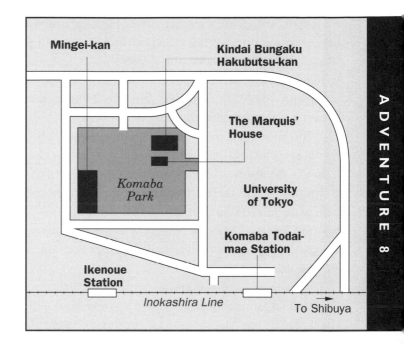

building, an architectural adaptation of a 150-year-old residence in the north of Japan, followed perhaps by a few minutes in the villa of Marquis Maeda (naval attaché to the Japanese Embassy in London before the war), is a pleasant way to pass an afternoon.

Take the Inokashira Line local from Shibuya to the second stop, Komaba Todai-mae (fare ¥130). Take the Todai Exit from the station. In front of you are the gate and clock tower of this western campus of Tokyo University, the pre-eminent institution of learning in this learning-besotted country. Go in if you like, but be forewarned that the campus is a shambles.

Mingei-kan is a ten-minute stroll from the station along a street that winds a bit through one of Tokyo's best-heeled suburbs. In the entranceway, slip into a pair of slippers and pay the ¥1,000 entrance fee at the little administrative office.

The museum was built to accommodate the folk-art collection of Soetsu Yanagi, a professor at Kyoto University, who traveled the country buying and cataloging the objects of everyday living which were on the verge of being lost or thrown away. In this way, Yanagi single-handedly founded the movement in Japan to preserve this country's craft heritage, and not a moment too soon. Now the Japanese come to Mingei-kan, the shrine to the folk craft movement, to marvel at the sensibilities of their forefathers.

The museum is small and designed with flair. The great sweeping staircase with wide oak banisters has a clock on the landing which chimes the hours. The showcases holding the artifacts are like pieces of furniture and there are comfortable old chairs and benches to sit on while you contemplate the wonders around you.

You will notice how subdued the colors are, how quiet. These are objects for the use of ordinary people, not high officials, so ostentation is out of place.

Before you leave, spend some time in the little museum shop. You might find something you would like to take away with you to remind you of what you have seen—a lacquer bowl or some cloth handwoven in a traditional pattern or perhaps a splendid *furoshiki*.

Nippon Mingei-kan (tel: 3467-4527) is located at 4-3-33 Komaba, Meguro-ku. Open 10 a.m. to 5 p.m. except Mondays.

Lunch? Back down the street toward the station you will find **Miyagawa**, a tiny little shop where you can have *unaju*, eel broiled over charcoal on a bed of rice for ¥1,200, made the old way. Miyagawa has only two small tables and a little tatami area, as it does most of its business by *demae*—taking orders from the neighborhood over the phone and delivering by bicycle. Miyagawa is closed Thursdays, though.

After lunch you might want to wander to nearby **Komaba Park** to visit the house of Marquis Maeda. Go right in; there's no admission charge. The main room is 50 tatami mats, which in Japanese terms makes it *huge*, and it is absolutely devoid of decoration of any kind. It looks out on a garden of rocks and carp pools and carefully groomed pines. Sit out on the little veranda and listen to the cawing of the crows.

PART TWO *The Metropolis*

*This enormous, sprawling city works for the most part
like clockwork, not because municipal authority
enforces a schedule but because those whose job it is to
keep the city functioning generally perform their jobs
with dispatch and dedication. To observe a gas station
attendant filling a car's gas tank or a train driver
checking that everything is in order after bringing his
train to the end of the line is to glimpse an everyday
brand of fanaticism.*

*The city is so deliciously varied. After living in
Tokyo for over a decade, I can walk the streets for
hours, enthralled. Indeed, anyone bored with Tokyo
is bored with life.*

Shinjuku is the busiest railway station in the world, with something like a million-and-a-half commuters scurrying through it every day. The Chuo and Yamanote railway lines (the two busiest in Japan by a good margin), the Keio, Odakyu, Saikyo, and Sobu lines (no slouches themselves), and the Marunouchi and Toei subway lines all empty into Shinjuku Station, which also manages to accommodate four built-in department stores.

As a good third of the day's people-moving activity takes place between 7:45 and 8:30 in the morning, to be in attendance during this period is to witness an astounding exercise in social organization.

The platform between Tracks 9 and 10 is the best vantage point. A safe place to position yourself so you won't be swept away is next to one of the water fountains in the middle of the platform. Looking up at the schedule which hangs over the platform, you will note that between 8 and 9 a.m., 22 Sobu Line trains are scheduled to arrive on Track 9, while Yamanote Line trains on Track 10 arrive so frequently that the times aren't even listed—the schedule simply notes that there will be a train every two to five minutes throughout the day.

In fact, during rush hour a ten-car Yamanote train carrying upward of three thousand people pulls into Track 10 every 90 seconds. At times, trains arrive at Tracks 9 and 10 simultaneously.

The scene is Dante-esque. By 8 o'clock the platform swarms with people—school kids in uniform, grandmothers in kimono, the middle-management cadre with their briefcases and morning papers, laborers with stubble on their chins. They line up four abreast in front of the marks on the platform which indicate where the doors will be. Railway police in Sam Browne belts whistle the stragglers into place, and two white-gloved JR train men station themselves at the head of each waiting phalanx in order to pry the doors open when the train comes in and to pack in the legs and elbows of those who otherwise wouldn't fit on the departing train.

A recorded voice oblivious to the hubbub announces, "Momentarily, the train for Harajuku and Shibuya will arrive on Track 10. Please stand back of the white line and be alert." Then, just to make sure that everybody has taken in this incantation (which is repeated a thousand times a day), a voluble train jockey in a booth overlooking the spectacle re-broadcasts exactly the same information. The din of whistles, alarms, proclamations, exclamations, warnings, and instructions is stupendous, but through it all the multitude waits in silence. (In the evening, on the way home, the atmosphere will be different: there will be chatter and laughter. But now, this is serious business. We are on our way to work!)

Peak crunch comes at about 8:10. A train rumbles in; and passengers tumble out—about 300 from each car—then seconds later the tide reverses and the waiting horde boards. A final few rugby players pitch themselves into the train at the last second. A young lad makes it but his girlfriend can't. A flag is waved, a whistle blown, and the train pulls out. It is traveling at full speed by the time the last car passes the end of the platform. Fifty people who couldn't squeeze on are already lined up at each marker waiting for the next train and the queue stretches completely across the platform, blocking traffic. The platform is filling up; people can't get to the stairs before the next train arrives. Miraculously, in the midst of it all, a station cleaner roams the platform sweeping up cigarette butts.

The whole machine teeters on the edge of breakdown as the allowable leeway in the arrival and departure times of these trains is just ten seconds. Occasionally there is a suicide. It is ordinarily cleaned up in less than ten minutes, but by then ten trains will be stacked up. As a deterrent, JR bills the family for the inconvenience.

By 8:45 this grand urban extravaganza with its cast of tens of thousands is over.

Sushi for Breakfast   10

A visit to **Tsukiji**, Tokyo's extraordinary fish market, offers an insight into how things work in this country. The routine of the place, even as it tiptoes lightly along the edge of chaos, is as tightly organized as a military invasion and everyone knows that they must work together or the whole thing will collapse.

Besides, a visit to Tsukiji is a lark. Tsukiji is open to anyone, and so it has the aspect of an Italian street fair, or rather a dozen Italian street fairs crammed into space for one. You go to Tsukiji as an adventurer, a seeker of early-morning exoticism, but such is the pace of business that no one has time to pay you the slightest attention, unless you happen to be in the way. Only toward the end of Tsukiji's day (around 8 in the morning), will things have slackened to the point that Tsukiji people will have time for a cup of tea or a can of beer and gentle jokes about your earnest curiosity.

"Where do those come from?" you ask, pointing to a tray of prickly black mollusks as big as softballs.

"From the sea, I suppose," says the grizzled stall owner with a wink. "Can't hardly find that sort of thing in the mountains anymore." In fact, as you find out later, the mollusks are found in only one place, off the coast of Ceylon, and they are available for sale at only one place in the world, right here. To the people who work here, Tsukiji—although it is the largest of Japan's 50 or so municipal markets and quite possibly the most sophisticated market in the world—is a perfectly ordinary place to work, and this in the end may be the most extraordinary thing about it.

A third of all the fish consumed in Japan (and Japan consumes a sixth of the world's fish) comes through Tsukiji—more than 2,500 tons a day. Such is the drawing power of the market that it is not unusual for a catch of high-grade fish taken off the coast of Kyushu to be iced and rushed to Tokyo to be sold the next morning to buyers representing a fish wholesaler *in Kyushu.* Tsukiji is as efficient as an electrical circuit. It can put a lobster crawling on the ocean floor off Gloucester, Massachusetts, on your plate in Tokyo in 24 hours.

The Central Wholesale Market (Tsukiji's formal name) stands on land reclaimed 300 years ago from Tokyo Bay. It occupies about as much space as the grounds of the football stadium of a large American university, but on an average day 17,000 trucks come and go through its two gates, to say nothing of the motorized battalions of motorcycles, bicycles, and solid-tired delivery carts that manage to fill any remaining gaps in the swarm of traffic.

The market is organized into tiers. Only seven old-established wholesaling companies called *niyuke* are authorized to buy directly from the boats. The *niyuke* sell to second-level wholesalers called *nakaoroshi*. Each of the 1,152 authorized *nakaoroshi*, most of whom specialize in a particular species of fish, is allotted just seven square meters of selling space under Tsukiji's great curving sheds, and the location of their stalls is changed by lot every four years in the interest of fairness.

(Try to imagine the unholy chaos that occurs when this happens and the sushi shops, local fish markets, and the general public all must search for the new location of their accustomed suppliers in a brand-new maze!) This tiered organization insures that fish change hands at least three times before they even leave the gates, but such is the secret of Tsukiji's efficiency.

The classic Tsukiji set piece is the tuna auction, which begins around 5 in the morning and continues until 6 or 6:30. Most of the tuna are frozen, because freezing doesn't significantly affect the taste of such a large, red-blooded fish, and hundreds of headless and tailless carcasses frozen as hard as bricks, some from as far away as New York and all dabbed with runes of red paint to indicate their weight and provenance, are laid out in rows on an open expanse of cold concrete out back by the river.

An eerie fog emanates from the frozen tuna as the gravel-voiced auctioneers get to work. Under the dim lights it seems the scene of an ancient druidical rite. The auctioneers communicate with the buyers in a series of smirks and twitches — ordinary language is too languid to sell a tuna every four seconds. The concentration of the auctioneers is so intense that sweat pours down their cheeks, even in the dead of winter.

Some *nakaoroshi* will buy four or five perfect specimens of tuna every day, which they take back to their stalls, cut up with long swords, and arrange under lights on a bed of ice, like diamonds. The very best tuna goes for ¥10,000 a kilo wholesale, six or seven times as expensive as premium beef.

Tsukiji handles about 400 species of fish, and most are kept alive in plastic tubs of running water (which is why everyone wears rubber boots) so they can be killed at the last possible moment, by a needle through the central nerve. It is felt that the taste of a fish which has been allowed to expire on its own is less well-defined.

The tendency for *nakaoroshi* to specialize can be bewildering. The amateur buyer inquires: "Where can I buy some crab?" only to be asked, "What kind? *Kegani? Zuai? Watari?*" Different *nakaoroshi* specialize in each type. The most expensive food sold at Tsukiji is *hamako-no-kodomo-no-hoshiteru*, dried sea-slug roe, at ¥100,000 a kilo. It is available through special *nakaoroshi* called *chinmiya*, who supply gourmet restaurants and drinking places. (I have no idea what it tastes like; pretty pungent I suppose.)

Tsukiji also sells vegetables (120,000 tons of cucumbers last year), plus fruit, meat, eggs, and pickles, as well as exotic comestibles, like *foie gras* and maple syrup, from 48 countries. Tsukiji has its own bookstore (stocked with books about fish), museum (of fishing), hotel, and public bath. If you are running a restaurant, you can buy your knives, uniforms, plates, scales, and chopsticks here.

You don't have to get up at the crack of dawn to see Tsukiji in action. If you get there by 6 a.m. you'll see whole operas. By then, Tsukiji's little shops are serving bowls of Chinese and Japanese noodles and selling buckets and fish gaffs and thick felt insoles to go inside boots. Tsukiji's rhythm is six hours out of phase with the rest of the city.

The vegetable auction, a slightly more relaxed affair than the pandemoniac tuna auction, begins at 7 o'clock. The two dozen or so auctioneers line up before the bleachers where the buyers have taken up their positions, and when the bell rings they doff their caps and bow, giving out a lusty *"Ohayo gozaimasu!"*

They all start selling at once, shoulder to shoulder—grapes as big as golf balls, apples as big as *boules*, and the fabulously expensive Japanese melons—the most pampered fruit in the world, fruit to be given away as gifts to the boss and to valued customers, fruit which has been grown and packaged with fanatical care.

The lots come in, are bid for and knocked down in seconds, and are whisked away by scurrying minions with flashlights tucked in their boots. Bags of chestnuts, mushrooms from Korea and Iwate Prefecture, *chingensai, myoga, konasu, ginnan nuts, yamatoimo,* fresh *wasabi*, and huge knuckles of new ginger; anything, everything, the best, the very best.

Tsukiji's writing instrument is the blunt felt-tip pen. Its effluvium is the broken shards of white styrofoam containers, which are bulldozed into mountains and compressed into evil-looking discs by the end of the day. The Tsukiji obbligato is the buzz of the band saw and the chatter of the marketplace: "Welcome, welcome! Only 800 yen. 800 yen! Going fast. How about it? Welcome, welcome!"

Tsukiji's buildings are of a Dickensian cast as the market has no time to think of renovation. Tsukiji is where you can see a huge frozen tuna slid across the cobblestone to act as a temporary doorstop.

There is something delightfully raffish about *sushi* for breakfast, like Champagne and strawberries. Sushi breakfast breaks the routine, jars you out of the tracks. A good place among many good places, for Tsukiji knows fish, is **Sushidai**, well known to everyone here. Sit at the counter and order *jo-zushi*, the top course for ¥2,500, then order à la carte as you fancy after that.

And here you are, right in the middle of Tokyo, wide awake and exhilarated at 8 a.m., with the whole day ahead of you. It's an easy walk to Shinbashi or the Ginza, passing people on their way to workaday jobs.

A Stroll Through Fashionable Tokyo

11

This walk, which begins with a promenade down Omotesando, the tree-lined boulevard which those with a romantic turn of mind like to think of as Tokyo's Champs Elysées, is best undertaken on a Sunday. To prepare, just slip on some comfortable walking shoes and, if you wish, make a reservation for Sunday brunch at L'Orangerie, which I'll describe later. The walk might take between four and five hours, leaving plenty of time to get sidetracked.

Take the Yamanote Line to Harajuku Station and exit this half-timbered ramshackle of a landmark by the Omotesando Exit, the exit nearest Shibuya. If you can manage to leave the station by 10:30, your timing for brunch will be *pittari* ("bang on the nose").

If the day is clear, you might like to see if you can spot Mt. Fuji from the span of the pedestrian bridge, but if not, stay on the side of the boulevard nearest the station for now. (On Sundays, the whole boulevard turns into a pedestrian mall from 1 to 5 p.m.)

Head down Omotesando. The trees are *keyaki*—Japanese elm. Thirty years ago this was a sedate part of town, but as you can see it has been heavily infiltrated by a ragged commercialism: jewelry peddlers who find the generous sidewalks accommodating, purveyors of *gelati* and pasta, sidewalk cafes, hairdressing establishments, chocolatiers, and pizza and hamburger factories. Young Tokyo is learning a new code of etiquette which sanctions the licking of an ice cream cone while strolling. The Quest Building, with its Ralph Lauren shop, its branch of Demel, Hofzuckerbacker (confectioner to the Viennese Court), and La Ranarita, the smart Milanese restaurant, is an attempt to keep the tone up.

Cross Meiji-Dori, one of the city's major arteries, and head up the gentle slope. Fashion houses are on the back streets all around you. The brooding ivy-covered apartments which stretch to the top of the slope on this side of the street, are the **Aoyama Apartments**. Tokyo's first stab at a new way of living in cities, the apartments were built in 1925 with a loan from a forward-looking Imperial princess. They are standing on extremely valuable real estate and, although they are now gently crumbling away, it seems to be practically impossible to get all 150 tenants to agree to sell at the same time so the apartments can be torn down and new ones put up. Nevertheless, the apartments are slowly being taken over by boutiques with great plate-glass windows: the effect is similar to that of neon signs in a castle.

Cross the street and window shop at **Paul Stuart**, clothes for the discreet dandy (and there is no dandy like a Japanese dandy), **Gallerie de Pop** with its flamboyant flower arrangement in the window, **Shu Uemura**, the high priest of makeup, **Peek-A-Boo**, the hair salon, and **Chez Toi**, the women's shop—*"La mode s'inspire de l'époque. Nous vous offrons une grande variété de créations qui vivent avec votre époque"* is inscribed in florid script on the door.

Brunch runs from 11 a.m. to 2:30 p.m. at **L'Orangerie** in the Hanae Mori Building. (You will have called M. Nozawa, the *maitre d'*, at 3407-7461 early in the week to tell him you are coming.) If you disdain the elevator and take the escalator to the fifth floor, you will wind your way up through a display of the current Hanae Mori collection—great blasts of *haute-couture* color, with shop attendants all in black. Here the wife of Mitsubishi France comes to buy the evening dress she will wear to the opening of the Paris Opera. It might cost $3,000 and be constructed of thousands of iridescent sequins all sewn by hand.

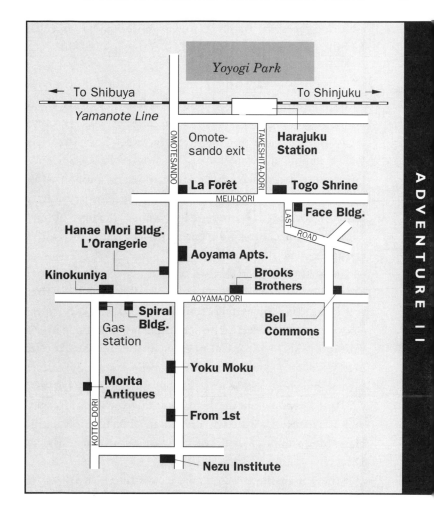

L'Orangerie is one of Tokyo's finest French restaurants and was inspired by L'Orangerie in Paris, one of Madame Mori's favorite places. Here the idea of brunch was introduced to Tokyo and it is here that you will still find the most elegant brunch in the city. It is served buffet-style, but a reservation gives you your own table, which is immaculately set as if brunch were the premier meal of the day. It is an eclectic spread, running from stuffed tomatoes to sushi,

imported cheeses to bagels, as well as more standard fare. The tariff is
¥3,500, and a bottle of Moët and Chandon is ¥12,000.

Now well-brunched, let us move on.

In the basement of the Hanae Mori Building is a collection of
antique shops, a fine place to browse for a bit to let brunch settle.
Ao sells antique indigo fabrics. **Idée** sells articles of "*intérieur
retro*," such as items for the dressing table. **Soul trip** sells baubles
Proust might have kept on his bedside table. Old telephones and
typewriters, lace chemises and teddy bears, monocles and signet
rings, fountain pens and art deco evening bags, Lalique glass and
cameo brooches, all studiously arranged. How about a 1900
Vacheron Constantin gold repeater pocket watch for ¥800,000? But
enough!

Cross Aoyama-Dori (known to motorists as Route 246) and turn
right. The **Spiral Building**, a fine example of the New Tokyo Architecture which is beginning to make itself felt in New York and Los
Angeles, presents itself for inspection. The building is worth a stroll-
through. Walk in and go around the atrium to the rear of the building. There is a good chance there will be an exhibit there which
breaks some sort of new ground. Mount the great spiral staircase in
the back and come out on the second floor, where a dozen very large
tables are spread with classy quotidian objects: tools and soaps and
glasses and ribbons—here you can buy a souvenir of the New Japan
Design.

Now out in the street again, to continue down Aoyama-Dori.
Turn left at the gas station across from **Kinokuniya**, which is to
Tokyo as Fauchon is to Paris. This street is informally called Kotto-
Dori, "The Street of Antique Shops." **Morita Antiques**, which spe-
cializes in antique textiles and folk art, is a particularly congenial
shop. The street is heavily stocked with ultra-smart boutiques like
Kenzo, where no piece of furniture would ever dare to intrude, and
Idée, where the couch is a sculptural object. You will see elegant
dogs on leashes and highly polished foreign motor cars of unusual
provenance.

Turn off Kotto-Dori to the left at **Matsushita Associates, Original Ukiyoe** (woodblock) **Prints**, which is, however, closed on Sundays.

This street also is closed to automobiles on Sundays. In the middle of the long wall running along the right-hand side of the street, you will discover the entrance to the **Nezu Institute of Fine Arts** (closed Mondays and the month of August).

It costs nothing to walk in the wonderfully landscaped garden with its two teahouses, carp lazing in deep pools, groves of bamboo and thick carpets of moss. It is miraculously quiet in the garden, save for the sound of trickling water, and the pace of your walk will slow to contemplation. It costs ¥500 to enter the museum itself, which is famous for its collection of massive Chinese bronzes and ormolu clocks built in the style of Fabergé Easter eggs for an emperor of the Ching Dynasty.

Now head back down toward Aoyama-Dori. You'll pass the **From 1st Building**, one of Tokyo's first buildings to be devoted solely to fashion, and **Yoku Moku**, whose courtyard is a favorite spot for cappuccino and a wedge of pastry.

At Aoyama-Dori, turn right. Across the street is **Brooks Brothers**, with its racks of brass-buttoned blazers and piles of cashmere pullovers. They're doing very well in Japan and have stores in Osaka and Sapporo.

A hundred meters beyond the solemn aisles of Brooks Brothers, at the Bell Commons Building, turn left onto "Killer-Dori." (There are many stories of how the street got its name, but nobody really knows, as the name is unofficial. Officially, it's Gaien Nishi-Dori.) This is yet another fashion street—with boutiques called **Barbiche, Madame, Nicole**, and **Peyton Place**. The **Watari-um** (Watari Museum of Contemporary Art), in its building by Mario Botta, is determinedly avant-garde. Its bookstores and stationery shop called **... on Sundays** specializes in art books and museum-quality postcards, some of photographs of old Japan. In the basement, a small espresso costs ¥400.

At a little faux-bucolic shop called **Afternoon**, which sells hand-crafted sweaters, turn left onto Last Road ("Lasto Rodo" in Japanese.) Here, there are still more boutiques: **K-Factory**, **Yestermorrow**, **Kid Blue Muse**, **Vazarely**, and **Zaftig**, although the names are always changing.

On the right, just as Last Road runs into Meiji-Dori, is the **Face Building**, another example of New Tokyo Architecture. Take a left here onto Meiji-Dori.

On the first and fourth Sunday of each month, a flea market is held on the grounds of Togo Shrine. There are hundreds of old silk kimono for ¥1,000 each, old leather suitcases with labels from around the world, trays of military buttons, antique pressed-tin advertisements, old toys and musical instruments—it's one of the city's best flea markets.

By now, all but the athletes among us will be beginning to wilt. We are now almost back to home base, Harajuku Station, but first we must traverse an obstacle course called Takeshita-Dori. Continue down Meiji-Dori until you see a building sporting a sign which says "Marron," and turn right there.

Takeshita-Dori is 200 meters long and jam-packed with teenagers from all over the country who come here to rig themselves out in frilly socks, lace collars, sunglasses, and striped tights—or whatever the extremely evanescent fashion of the moment may be—and to eat crepes and have their hair cut the way the teen magazines suggest. It's going to take you 20 minutes to fight your way up this short street, but this is triple-distilled Tokyo and too much a part of this crazy city to miss.

And at the end of Takeshita-Dori is the lower exit of Harajuku Station.

Asakusa and the *Shitamachi* Spirit 12

Board the Ginza Line, perhaps at its Shibuya terminus, and ride to the last stop, Asakusa. The Ginza Line, the oldest subway in the city, touches all bases as it winds its way through the city, from oh-so-smart Omotesando to big business Toranomon to Fifth-Avenue Ginza to bustling, cut-rate Kanda to down-home Ueno.

The Ginza Line was built when Tokyo was on a different power system than it is now and the main lights will go off and the little light fixtures on the wall of the car will flicker on when there is a momentary transition between the new power system and the old. To travel thus from one end of the city to the other costs ¥230.

When you emerge, you will be less than a minute from Kaminarimon ("Thunder Gate"), the entrance to Senso ji, the temple of the Goddess of Mercy, founded 1,200 years ago and now easily Tokyo's most famous tourist attraction for foreigners and Japanese alike. All of Japan views the Asakusa area, of which Senso-ji is the centerpiece, as the embodiment of *shitamachi* ("downtown") Tokyo. By contrast, the Ginza is just glitter.

At Kaminarimon, with its fierce wooden statues guarding a huge ragged red lantern, the tourist buses double park and groups arrange themselves for ritual photographs. Pitchmen jockey for the best position to sell balloons and bubble-blowing machines and *ramune,* old-fashioned ginger ale in a bottle sealed with a glass marble. You stand here in the sentimental epicenter of Tokyo, indeed, of all Japan.

You will be drawn down the long promenade of dozens of shops called *nakamise* which leads up to the temple itself. These shops sell everything for everybody, from Frankenstein and Noh masks to exceedingly rococo wedding dresses, from umbrellas of oiled paper (¥2,000) to intricate decorations for the wigs worn with full ceremonial kimono, scarves emblazoned with maps of the Tokyo subway system (¥300), gift boxes of exotic handmade candies to be sampled

during a tea ceremony, racks of the white patent-leather shoes favored by gangsters and those who would like to be thought of as such
(50 years ago this same shop sold wooden *geta*), plastic samurai
swords, regiments of battery-powered drum-beating bears, patent
medicines to relieve every known infirmity, trays of eyeglasses, glossy
pictures of movie stars, antique armor, kamikaze headbands (¥300)
to be worn while studying for big exams, and an overwhelming variety of souvenir trinkets and just plain junk.

It is 42nd Street, Coney Island, Portobello Road, and Tivoli rolled
into one and raised to the fifth power, a scene of unbridled capitalism,
where pigeons and picture-takers, fortune tellers, wistful lovers, mis-
placed children, monks mumbling sutras over their wooden begging
bowls, gaggles of ladies in mourning black who have come in com-
memoration (and later to picnic), and street touts selling glass-cutting

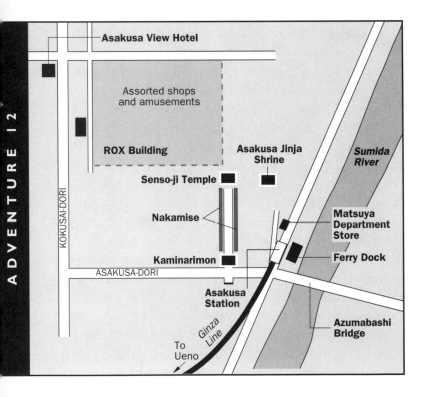

ADVENTURE 12

Asakusa View Hotel

Assorted shops
and amusements

ROX Building

KOKUSAI-DORI

Asakusa Jinja
Shrine

Sumida
River

Senso-ji Temple

Nakamise

Matsuya
Department
Store

Kaminarimon

Ferry Dock

ASAKUSA-DORI

Asakusa
Station

Ginza Line

Azumabashi
Bridge

To
Ueno

knives and tips on the winner of the third race at Fuchu all circulate serenely as if at one great neighborhood clam bake.

"What is the purpose of all this?" asks an earnest young tourist of her guide, who bursts out in amazed laughter. "You ask me the purpose of *life?*"

Pick your way through the *nakamise* shops toward Senso-ji. Scattered around the sprawling grounds, which are meant to evoke a spacious Buddhist heaven, there are a dozen pocket pavilions celebrating, for example: Bensai-ten, the Goddess of the Creative Arts (who also doubles as the Goddess of Money-making); Jizo, the Spirit of Ambition in Children; and Awashima-do, which commemorates the faithful service of needles and pins. Systematic theology it is not.

Go up the broad steps into the temple, right to the altar. Toss a coin into the immense wooden offertory box, clap your hands to catch the attention of a drowsy deity, and be quiet for a few seconds. You can walk right around the temple on its wide porch, and sit on the porch and write a letter, read the paper, feed the pigeons, doze.... Senso-ji is open to the public. Kids in a contemplative mood ride their motorcycles right up to the steps. Here solemnity is scarce.

The smaller Asakusa Jinja (shrine) off to the right is less frequented and quieter. Take off your shoes to enter its tatami expanse. A priest is usually in attendance and he might offer you tea. This is the site of the incredibly boisterous Sanja Festival in May, Tokyo's version of Mardi Gras. Each year over a million people attend to dance and sway and shout and feel part of *shitamachi*. At the end of August, a knockdown drag-out Samba Festival with dancers from Brazil takes off from here to wend its way through the area in a long snake dance.

Adjacent to Senso-ji is an area of back streets worth wandering down for a glimpse of a wonderfully varied urban landscape now in the throes of a fitful transition. Here is the sleek new Asakusa View Hotel—28 stories and visible from everywhere; the Rockza, the last remaining strip-show theater of the dozens that used to line Rokku Cinema Street; a surfeit of pachinko parlors; an off-Broadway kabuki theater (¥1,000 admission); several *rakugo* (comic monologue) theaters which are very much alive; a six story off-track betting emporium and the pawnshops to go with it; a clutter of shops which sell clothes *very* cheaply (a pair of trousers for ¥700, for example); a community bath house (entrance ¥500) at which the locals stage amateur vaudeville after their baths just for the hell of it; and the ROX Building (New Tokyo Architecture at its most spectacular), which comprises among other divertissements a wedding hall and a swimming pool.

Asakusa is under assault by interests who wish to upgrade the area, to build riverside parks and sports palaces and new bridges across the Sumida River. Everywhere there are signs of the battle between the old and the new. Which side are you on?

But enough. It is better to come back another day than to try to fix Asakusa in your mind too quickly. It will resist any attempt to pigeonhole it, and you will see it in a different way when you come again. So let us go.

I expect you are hungry. Go back to Kaminarimon and from there to Matsuya Department Store. In the basement you will be able to buy a nice *bento* lunch box and something to drink with it. The whole shouldn't cost more than ¥2,000. Then cross the street to the Sumida River Ferry and buy a ¥920 ticket to Hamarikyu. You will be given two tickets, one of which will gain you entrance to Hamarikyu Imperial Garden at the mouth of the river, 30 minutes away.

There is a ferry every 45 minutes, and it is sure to be crowded. This is Tokyo, after all. But the trip down the Sumida is worth the wait and the jostle. Each bridge is a different structural approach to the problem of spanning an expanse of water, so the trip is an exhibition of these bridges as well as highways, trains, slow-moving barges, and huge neon signs. Around the last bend you will see Tokyo Tower in the distance. Soon you dock and are let out into Hamarikyu Garden. The park is the loveliest in Tokyo, a former Imperial duck shoot with a pond in the middle that rises and falls with the tide. You can have your *bento* here on benches and a table, or sit on the grass.

The city peeps out above the edges of the park, but is far away. Walk through the park, across the bridge over the pond, past the teahouse in the middle of the bridge (the teahouse can be rented for your own private party, but that is another Little Adventure), to the exit. Shinbashi Station on the Yamanote Line is a 15-minute walk away.

The *Shitamachi* Spirit: Old Edo Thumbs Its Nose

Old Tokyo was divided into a downtown and an uptown. Downtown lay in the flat lands east of the Sumida River and was made up of neighborhoods which by all accounts overflowed with a joyous zest for living. Shitamachi, *literally "low town," was where the plain man of Tokyo—the real* Edokko—*lived. Uptown was on the bluff, the rising land which is now encircled by the Yamanote Line. Yamanote people were the aristocrats, the administrators, those with position and rank.*

Every city has its core of honest, lively, open-hearted unpretentious citizenry, who are often seen in contrast to the elevated souls, somehow less part of the city, who live in the mews and around the tree-lined boulevards. New York has its Brooklynites, London its Cockneys, and Rome its denizens of Trastevere. But the people who lived in Tokyo's shitamachi *seem to have been something more than just the city's colorful commoners. There seems to have been a* shitamachi *spirit, which is, however, hard to pin down—it is utter lack of pretension and a love of life infused with a cosmic cunning—but there's a story which seems to come close to the heart of it.*

It happened that a good-natured rivalry arose between the people of Yamanote and the people of shitamachi *as to which section of the city harbored the citizen with the most extraordinary tattoo. At the time, tattooing was an intricate art practiced by diligent craftsmen who could command considerable commissions.*

The citizens of Yamanote, after appropriate consultations, decided who among themselves should represent Yamanote in the grand tattoo face-off, and the shitamachi *people huddled and in their own chaotic and boisterous way managed finally to settle on who should represent them. And so it was arranged that one evening the two champions would meet in a teahouse overlooking the Sumida River before a panel of judges and it would be decided who in fact had the more extraordinary tattoo, after which the Yamanote people would return to their task of governing and the* shitamachi *people would get back to their job of being governed.*

After cups of tea and a period of polite conversation, the head judge nodded to the citizen from Yamanote, who stood up and let his silk kimono fall from one shoulder. The light in the room seemed to shimmer as he unveiled a brilliant depiction of a golden dragon from whose nostrils flared a flickering flame. On careful inspection, the judges found the tattoo's detail miraculous, as though it had been engraved by a diamond. The judges thanked the citizen of Yamanote, who could not suppress a smile, for after all one has few occasions to exhibit one's tattoo in public if one does not frequent the public baths, which, of course, the citizen of Yamanote never did.

The head judge then nodded to the man from shitamachi, *who walked to the center of the room and let his simple cotton summer kimono slide off his left shoulder. There was no tattoo to be seen. Then he undid his sash and took his kimono off. Nothing. There was not a tattoo anywhere on the rough, weather-beaten body of the man from* shitamachi. *The judges looked at each other, puzzled.*

Then the man took off his fundoshi *loincloth and stood naked in the center of the room. But still, no tattoo.*

Then our man peeled back his foreskin and there on the tip of his member, the most sensitive part of any man's body, was the perfect realization of a tiny mosquito.

The Yokohama Waterfront   13

What we will do is this:

1. Take a ride on the world's largest Ferris wheel.
2. Stroll through the old commercial district of Yokohama and through Yamashita Park, Yokohama's waterfront public garden.
3. Visit the lobby of a wonderful old hotel which has hardly changed at all since about 1927.
4. Take a water-bus back to the world's largest department store and Yokohama Station.

From Shibuya take the Toyoko Line (also called the Tokyu Line) to Sakuragi-cho, two stops beyond Yokohama. It costs ¥300 and takes 45 minutes by local train, 36 minutes by express.

As you come into Sakuragi-cho Station you'll see on the left *Nihon Maru*, the Japanese navy's fully rigged training ship, and the **Cosmo-clock**, a Ferris wheel with a 100-meter diameter, which is a couple of meters larger than Vienna's famous Ferris wheel, just as Tokyo Tower is a few meters taller than the Eiffel tower. Head for the Cosmoclock, so called because when it is lit up at night it tells the time. (Note, however, that Cosmoclock is closed Mondays.) You'll find yourself funneled into a "People Mover" moving sidewalk. Off to your left is the splendid new Yokohama Museum of Art, opened in 1989. The museum has no collection of its own yet; everything on display has been lent by wealthy Yokohama patrons of the arts.

It costs ¥600 to ride the Cosmoclock. A revolution takes 15 minutes and the ride is remarkably smooth. That beautiful bridge is the new Yokohama Bay Bridge. If it's clear, you can even see Mt. Fuji.

This whole vast area right under you is the Minato Mirai development project. It used to be a Mitsubishi shipyard, but it has been cleared for the development of new housing, offices, hotels, shopping malls, concert halls, theaters, parks, and a sports stadium over the next ten years. Actually, Yokohama is not the only city to have discovered that it has a waterfront ripe for growth: Tokyo, Osaka, Kobe, and Fukuoka also have large waterfront projects on the boards. European and American architects are heavily involved in all these projects and the results promise to be dazzling.

After nimbly alighting from the Ferris wheel, head back to Sakuragi-cho Station. Go out the front of the station, turn left and cross over Benten Bridge. Follow the signs pointing the way to Yamashita Park. You'll pass by the somber, classical facades of the old Yokohama banks and shipping companies on streets shaded by plane trees. Yokohama is Japan's second largest city but it is so much in the shade of Tokyo that it has a provincial feeling to it. Traffic seems desultory compared with Tokyo's. There are mansard roofs and cobblestones and gaslight lanterns. The weathered sign of a hostel says "Welcome Seamen."

Yamashita Park fronting the harbor has rose trellises, beds of tulips, fountains, and cast-iron benches. It looks like pre-war Lisbon. The illusion is further enhanced by the *Hikawa Maru*, the last of the Japanese ocean liners, built in 1920 and now docked here permanently. The

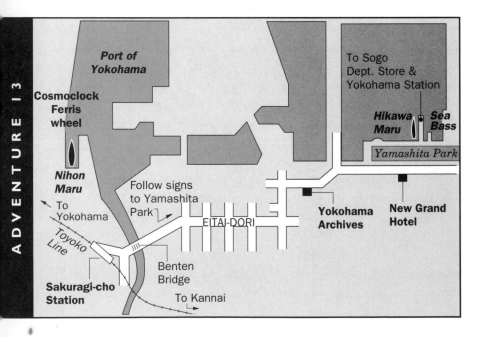

boarding fee is ¥800. You might like to take a look at the lobby of the **New Grand Hotel** across the street. The hotel was built in 1927 and even after a recent renovation its second-floor lobby is wonderfully evocative of old Yokohama, with comfortable overstuffed chairs, writing desks, local dailies on split bamboo rods, and large windows overlooking the street, like a London club.

If you linger in the lobby you might see an *omiai*, a meeting between a young man and a young woman arranged by a go-between for the purpose of determining if the chemistry is right for marriage. At any rate, there is apt to be a high incidence of formal kimono, as the New Grand is a favorite place for receptions. Every year for as long as anyone can remember, Yokohama high schools have brought their graduating classes to the New Grand for an elaborate Western meal and instruction in how to handle silverware according to Western etiquette.

After lunch you may be prepared to wander back. Consider returning to Yokohama Station by a water-bus called the *Sea Bass*, which leaves every 20 minutes from its pier next to the *Hikawa Maru*. Buy a ticket from Window 1 for ¥600.

You'll dock at **Sogo**, the world's largest department store. Descend to floor B2, Sogo's amazing food floor, and go right through to the exit on the opposite side. Keep going and you'll come to Yokohama Station. From here you can go back to Tokyo Station on JR or back to Shibuya on the Toyoko Line.

Note: Just as this edition went to press, the world's largest Ferris wheel was dismantled and stowed away. It will be re-erected on some site along the waterfront, an area now in the grips of a massive construction project involving a dozen new buildings, including, in Landmark Tower, the highest building in Japan. You have a glimpse here of what the new Tokyo is going to look like.

14   *Depaato* Opening and a Picnic on the Palace Moat

Japanese department stores cater to the whole person: they'll sell you a house along a railway line they just happen to own and an exotic foreign automobile with the steering wheel on the left to put in the garage. They'll teach you how to arrange flowers, how to wear the kimono, and how to scuba dive—in a pool with an underwater window that looks out on a street full of gawkers. They'll make a writing brush out of the residue of your baby's first haircut and will be happy to outfit him or her in the uniform of the elementary school of your choice. When you can't take it anymore, they'll sell you a ticket to their own resort in Sri Lanka, travel insurance included.

On the seventh floor of any Tokyo department store there will be exhibitions like English Landscape Painting, Sculpture of Equatorial Africa, and Hitherto Unknown Photographs of Marilyn Monroe, complete with lavishly illustrated catalogs. There will be free clinics on how to recognize signs of rheumatism and gout, and advice on cooking and diet in a world of tantalizing choices. They will inspect your teeth in their own dental clinic, repair your shoes while you wait, print your wedding invitations, and arrange for your funeral. They'll make up silk underwear to measure and sell you an entire crocodile skin from which you can then have items made to desire—a cowboy belt? A wallet to your own secret design? Ski boots? One Tokyo department store (Seibu in Ikebukuro) runs an on-premise college for its customers and has one of the finest collections of cheeses you are likely to come across anywhere in the world.

Mitsukoshi department store in Nihonbashi opened its doors in 1673 as a shop selling kimono. Mitsukoshi is a model of its type and perhaps the most august department store of them all. It is instructive to observe the little ritual that proceeds the opening of the doors at Mitsukoshi, a ritual that takes place every day at 10 a.m. sharp, except on Mondays when the store is closed.

Mitsukoshi has its own subway station, Mitsukoshi-mae on the Ginza Line, the city's oldest subway line. Take Exit A5 from the station and go right around the corner to the entrance with a large bronze lion on either side. There are chairs to sit on while you wait. It is a kind of club for early morning Mitsukoshi shoppers, who may number 50 at this entrance alone by the time the doors swing open.

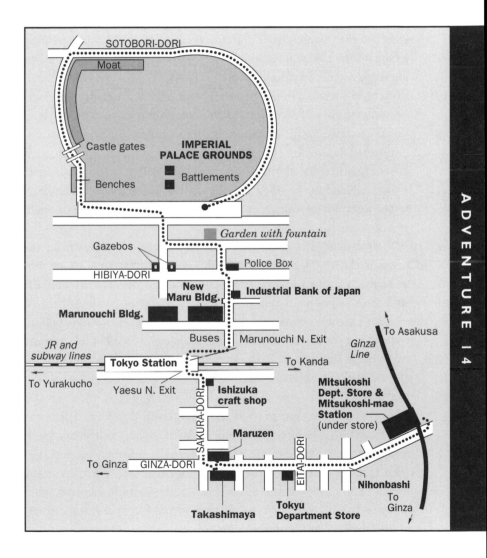

At 9:45 you can see through the glass a platoon of 40 shopgirls in Mitsukoshi uniform assembling to receive their daily instructions from their (male) section chief. He will demonstrate a new product, point out a new display, read a communication from on high, and answer any questions. This is the morning *chorei*, the daily meeting of the primary group which takes place in one form or another in all Japanese organizations. It is the time for the section leader to tell everyone that Ikuko-san is going to take her one-week vacation in Italy and that Sumie-chan's grandmother in Fukuoka has passed away so she will be absent for a while. The *chorei* ends with everyone bowing briskly to the section manager.

At 9:55 there is a flutter of announcements to the customers waiting outside about the various exhibitions, lectures, and demonstrations scheduled for the day and at 9:59 two guides in their own smart uniforms, chosen for their beauty and congeniality, take up their posts on either side of the doors. The dark-suited section managers stand back and to the side. The guides bow to each other, then bow to the assembly of waiting customers, then swing open the doors in perfect unison.

Chimes mark the hour and there are Handelian chords from the organ in the loft over the central hall, where resides the fantastic ten-meter-high statue of Magokoro, the Goddess of Sincerity and Patroness of Department Stores.

As the customers stream in, the shopgirls at their stations behind the counters bow and murmur, *"Irasshaimase"*—"welcome"—to any customer in sight, until the organ decrescendos, which is the signal to all employees to stop bowing *en masse* and get on with the business of the day.

The best way to go through the Mitsukoshi Building, which was completed in 1914 and was equipped with Japan's first escalator, is first to pick up a store guide in English at the information desk and then take the elevator to the eighth floor roof and work your way down. (The elevator ride is a Little Adventure in itself, elevator ladies being a Tokyo character type all their own, with their own superpolite language and butterfly diction.)

You can easily spend hours wandering around this amazing store, wondering how it could be that all of the consumer touchstones of the West, the Tiffanys, the Cartiers, the Fortnum & Masons and Gieves & Hawkes, plus all those of the East, could be assembled here so matter-of-factly under one roof.

Around noon, you may decide you have had enough. Exit onto the main street called here Ginza-Dori (the same street in the Ginza is called Chuo-Dori), and turn right. In short order you'll pass over the marvelously ornate Nihonbashi, the "Bridge of Japan," from which all distances from Tokyo are traditionally measured. In the 19th century, Nihonbashi was where young blades would take their girlfriends for a stroll through the Ginza, but as you see, the bridge's baroque lamp standards have been beheaded by the expressway overhead. It seems a monstrous joke, this product of the panicky construction period leading up to the 1964 Tokyo Olympics.

As you're walking this way, you might like to drop in on **Maruzen**, Tokyo's premier bookseller. (Maruzen is closed Sundays, though, a schedule which would be unthinkable for a department store.) Maruzen's first floor is a good display of general-interest Japanese books and magazines. The second is English-language paperbacks, textbooks, and books about Japan. The third is golfing gear and silk neckties. The fourth is a very good collection of books for children and a fine selection of art books and books about automobiles, motorcycles, yachts, ocean liners, wine, travel, and fashion, plus an art gallery, a craft shop with a modern sensibility (recall the shop of the Museum of Modern Art in New York), and the Maruzen Library of Books on Books, where you'll find books and journals about the making and publishing of books. Maruzen's basement houses the world's greatest collection of instruments for writing, including fountain pens from all over the world and, should you require, a selection of quill pens.

Perhaps by now you are feeling peckish? A remedy is to cross Ginza-Dori and descend to the basement of **Takashimaya**, another of Tokyo's top-line department stores. In Takashimaya's basement you can buy a box lunch put up for you by Alois Dallmayr, the famous Munich delicatessen, or by Peck, the famous ditto from Milan, or by The Silver Palate, whose main store is on Columbus Avenue, New

York City. It will cost less than ¥1,000. You might like to add a raspberry tart baked less than an hour previously by Fauchon of Paris, who will also sell you a bottle of stout Belgian beer or a bottle of Bordeaux if you like. Or you might like to pick up instead a Japanese bento lunch for ¥600 to ¥2,000, which is what a large number of Ginza office workers do.

Then follow the map through Tokyo Station to one of the two little stone gazebos on the palace moat or, if the gazebos have too recently been visited by pigeons, cross the bridge to the public garden behind the moat, with its fountain and pavilion and wooden benches. If you arrive after 1 o'clock the stockbrokers and office ladies will have drifted back to their offices.

After lunch you may be in the mood for walking it off. Consider walking completely around the Imperial Palace grounds on the outside of the moat, along Sotobori-Dori—"Outside Moat Street." It's exactly five kilometers and should take about an hour. You'll pass by the National Diet, the bunker-like Supreme Court Building, the National Theater (as simple a piece of architecture as imaginable), the Wacoal Building, made of plastic so that it sounds like a canoe when you thump it, the National Archives (small, because it is the habit of this country to commit only the most officious communications to paper), the Crafts Gallery of the National Museum of Art (looking like a French convent), the National Museum of Art itself, and the offices of the *Mainichi Shinbun* newspaper. You'll be kept company by a constant stream of glassy-eyed joggers.

Then back to Tokyo Station and the Yamanote Line.

PART THREE Tokyo Bizarro

Long-time Tokyo resident Donald Richie has observed that the Disneyland on Tokyo Bay is de trop—Tokyo is its own Disneyland. Picture this: the facade of this pachinko parlor is a four-story neon masterpiece flashing in all the color of benign terror, with the recorded clash of a brass band playing patriotic American tunes as a kind of counterpoint and a staff whose sole job is to announce in hysterical tones the numbers of the machines paying off at the moment. But the pachinko parlor's manager feels his establishment is not making a proper statement, so he hires a band in comic costumes and with twice the paraphernalia of a New Orleans jazz ensemble to stand out front to perform street theatricals in order to distract and attract passersby. Tokyo loves chaos, as long as it doesn't get out of hand.

Pachinko Fever 15

Pachinko is as much a part of life in Tokyo as slot machines are in Las Vegas. There can't be many Tokyoites who have never risked a few hundred yen in a pachinko parlor, of which Tokyo has over 1,500.

Foreigners peering into a pachinko parlor for the first time are always taken aback by the din: the slur of thousands of steel balls swirling through the system, the blare of a Sousa march, the over-amplified announcements that MACHINE 136 HAS JUST CAUGHT FEVER!!! (Earnest visitors from China have been known to ask what pachinko parlors are manufacturing that makes so much noise.) It is the chaos of combat, another world.

Not only are foreigners apt to be stunned by the fury of a pachinko parlor in full cry, but when they observe hundreds of pachinko players crammed together shoulder to shoulder, staring with maniacal intensity at the vertical pinball machines only inches from their noses, they are tempted to conclude that they have stumbled onto something uniquely, weirdly Japanese.

A self-styled explicator of The Japanese Mind once declared that it was impossible to understand Japan without understanding pachinko. This is, of course, the most awful humbug. Pachinko is gambling, and its ubiquitous presence makes Tokyo the gamblingest city in the world. (Total annual pachinko revenues are ¥13 trillion. Compare this with the total value of all video tape recorders produced in Japan in 1991 of ¥3 trillion.) Pachinko is popular because it offers, at little cost, a momentary escape from a workaday world, not because it puts people in a zen-like trance.

But it is true that if you disdain pachinko parlors because you see them as somehow vulgar, you deny yourself an experience that is uniquely Japanese. The game has never caught on outside Japan, despite several attempts to export it. The great deterrent for foreigners is that the game seems impossibly arcane. Read the next few paragraphs and you will know as much about general strategy as all but the *pachipros*—the pachinko professionals who live off of the game. Whatever analysts of The Japanese Mind may say, it is true that until you have bankrupted a pachinko machine you can never understand the deepest inner yearnings of a true Tokyoite.

How to Play the Game

1. **Pick your parlor.** In the past, there was some evidence that the odds were fractionally better at neighborhood pachinko parlors than at parlors located near the major stations. The rationale was that the local parlors had to cater to a fixed clientele which would not keep coming back unless they felt they were being given a reasonable shot at the jackpot, while the more centrally located parlors catered to a transient clientele who never really got to know the parlor. This potential edge no longer exists, however, as both parlors and players, and the game itself, have become more sophisticated.

Now the odds offered by parlors are very similar, although those which have just opened will initially adjust their machines for more generous payoffs in order to establish as quickly as possible the essential aura of action. One occasionally comes across a parlor which has managed to attract just a few customers, even during the peak playing hours of noon to 1 and 6 to 8. These eerie places are best avoided.

For the beginner as well as for the pro, the best parlors to play in are the most popular ones, assuming they are not so crowded that you cannot have a reasonable pick of machines. Two flagship parlors are the **Shinjuku New Tokyo**, which has the highest turnover in the city, and the **New Miyako Center**, which with 500 seats (the legal limit in Tokyo) is the city's largest. Both parlors are at the West Exit of Shinjuku Station.

Novelty parlors—such as the **26 Go-Sen** in Musashi Koyama, which has a concert hall where players in a slump can retire to wait it out, and the **Sequoia** in Nakano, where hostesses roam the aisles offering fruit juices, bonbons and encouragement—are not in favor with experienced pachinko players, who tend to be suspicious of embellishments. Still, if you feel fastidious, you may find that the elegant new **Jumbo** off Miyasuzaka near Shibuya Station is worth a visit: it is immaculate and provides hot *oshibori* (hand towels) at the end of play.

2. **Pick your time.** Payday in Japan is the 25th of the month. Just before payday the parlors tend to be more generous than usual in order to encourage players with only a smattering of loose change left in their pockets. Similarly, after a weekend or a long holiday, the machines tend to be more generous.

It is instructive to line up outside a parlor at ten in the morning. When the doors open, the *pachipros* (it is said that each parlor supports two or three professionals) will rush down the banks of machines in search of a soft touch. You are not likely to be able to judge the ripeness of a machine with the same practiced eye, however, and you will find that after the machines have been in play for several hours it will be more apparent which machines are more likely to pay off. Particularly good times to put in an appearance, for reasons explained below, are 1, 6 and 8 p.m. It is also said that a sudden afternoon rainstorm following a hot, dry morning can warp the plywood in the back of the machines in such a way that the odds are raised in favor of the players, but I suspect this is just another example of the extensive folk analysis to which pachinko has been subjected over the years.

3. **Pick your machine.** It is a pachinko maxim that a fool can win on the right machine but that even a pachinko genius cannot win on the wrong one. There are essentially four types of machines currently in play, although the three major manufacturers are very inventive, putting dozens of new variations on the market each year. (We will shortly see a whole new approach to the game when the manufacturers incorporate video discs, computer circuitry, and voice reproduction.)

Beginners should get their feet wet on *hikoki* ("airplane") type machines, which are designed to provide maximum action per ¥100 investment in 25 balls. Although they do not pay off as spectacularly as some other types of machines, these offer the best odds for players who have not taken the time to memorize a long sequence of numbers and who do not have the reflexes of a world-class Ping Pong player (as is required to win on the *digipachi*, "digital pachinko," machines which incorporate a slot machine).

The *hikoki* ("airplane") machine is so called because when a ball falls into one of the three cups at the bottom of the board marked "1" or "2," the "wings" open up for one or two intervals of 0.7 seconds. In order to make a machine "catch fever," that is, to start its 1,300-ball maximum payoff (the legal limit for this type of machine), it is necessary to slip a ball into the center V-Zone while the wings are open. Once you do this the full payoff is pretty assured, although if by some awful miscalculation you do not manage the comparatively easy task of feeding seven more balls into the V-Zone during the period while the wings are opening and closing, the fever will stop and the payoff will be reduced.

Every parlor has at least one bank of *hikoki* machines. They are the parlor's *asobidai*, the machines designed to attract average players, although some *pachipros* do specialize in these machines. Within this bank of machines, how do you locate the machines most likely to pay off? The *pachipros* do it by analyzing the alignment of key pins, sometimes with a gauge but more often just by eyeballing the machines; the process is very complex and takes considerable experience.

It is better for you to pick your machine simply by tracking its recent history. Machines that have paid out at least once during the day are hung with a sign which says *"Kaihodai"*—"Liberated (winning) Machine." In the absence of other evidence, one of these machines is what you want, if you can find one not already in play. Machines which have paid off at least once and which management suspects of being too generous have a *"Uchidomedai"* ("Bankrupted Machine") sign hung on them.

In order to drum up business, the parlor will often, at 1 and 8 and sometimes at 6 p.m., turn the *Uchidomedai* machines, which are not playable, into *Kaihodai* machines, which are. At these hours, players looking for a sure thing line up at the administrative desk in the back of the parlor so they may slip into a seat before one of these proven machines. Relatively few players actually resort to this strategy, because it is considered too timid for a real pachinko player. Most players prefer to take a chance on their ability to spot nail clearances themselves in order to zero in on a hot machine.

If you have established that a particular machine has a record of paying off, you might want to make a note of it, even though, particularly in neighborhood parlors, the nails may be realigned overnight by a *kugi-shi* ("nail doctor"), a professional nail adjuster. Machines in more centrally located parlors tend to have their nails adjusted less frequently.

4. **Play the odds**. Now that you have seated yourself before a potentially winning machine, buy ¥300 worth of balls and put them in your upper tray.

Look carefully at the nails immediately above the three lower cups and determine if either the left or the right "1" cups have a particularly inviting space between the nails. Turn the shooting control clockwise until balls start shooting up to the top of the machine. Aim for the left or right side for the top row of nails (*ten-kugi* or "heavenly nails"), depending on whether you have a better shot at the right or left "1" cup. Observe the fall of the balls and make adjustments as seems appropriate, but note that variations in the voltage as well as irregularities in the balls themselves will insure that the balls fall in a variety of patterns—you will have to play the odds.

You should hit a lower cup or one of the side "tulips" at least five times for your ¥300 worth of balls, for a payoff of 13 balls each time. If you manage to do this, and if you have picked a machine which keeps the balls in play above the wings (so that when the wings open there's a better chance of cascading a ball into the V-Zone), it's probably worth another ¥300 to check the machine out more thoroughly.

If the machine you have chosen is not generous to this extent, be prepared to move to another.

When you have bankrupted your machine, take your plastic container full of steel balls to the administrative desk to have them counted. You can claim a prize if you like, although you are unlikely to find anything sufficiently memorable to mark the occasion—the prizes are household articles like soap, toothpaste, towels, and cigarettes (it is said that 20 percent of the cigarettes produced in Japan are given away as pachinko prizes) to take home to appease the spouse.

More thrilling (because it's semi-illegal) is a payoff in cash: when you turn in the balls, let it be know that you prefer to be paid in "*genkin*." You will be given some markers and told to go down a nearby alley, climb a dark staircase, and present yourself at a small window in a steel door. Push your markers through the window and your booty will be slid out in exchange.

16   Finlando Sauna

There are various ways to experience the classic Japanese bath. You could bathe outdoors in a natural hot spring bubbling out of the depths of an ancient mountain, with the snow falling all around you and a warm beaker of saké floating on a tray at your elbow. Or you could bathe with a companion at a country inn in a tub constructed of silky *hinoki* wood, with slices of the delicate citrus called *yuzu* floating on the water to soften it and make it fragrant.

Or you could wander down to gaudy old Kabuki-cho for a languid soak at **Finlando Sauna**, the largest, the most efficient, and certainly the most inventive of Tokyo's ten thousand or so bathing establishments.

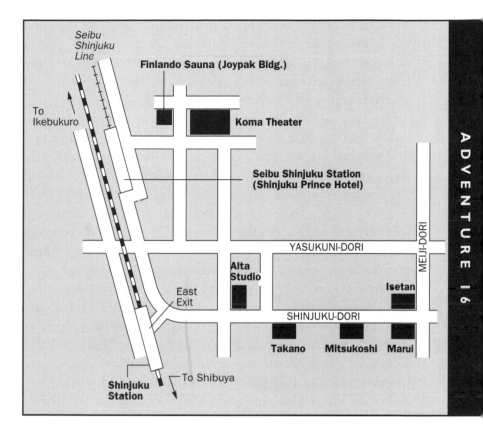

The place is easy to find. It's right across from the Kabuki-cho police box. You wind down a rather operatic staircase, slip off your shoes and deposit them in a locker. Pay a maximum of ¥7,750 (depending on the time of day), which includes an excellent massage. (It's a maximum of ¥2,800 without the massage but with all the time in the bath you like.) You will be guided to your locker by an attendant well-versed in dealing with befuddled foreigners and bumpkins from the provinces.

Finlando Sauna is a bath machine.

Strip, stow your duds, wrap a peach-colored towel around your middle and descend the stairs to the steam rooms.

Steam Room Number One is spacious and carpeted. There is a television set built into the wall, tuned to a program which requires little concentration. Maybe five or ten minutes here, just to open the pores. Next a tiled room where, when you hit a button, you are skewered by bracing jets of water from all directions.

Then on to Steam Room Number Two. You are beginning to loosen up. When you are ready for relief, retreat from the heat and dive into the mini Olympic swimming pool ringed with palm trees and dignified with statuary, with a jacuzzi spitting out of one corner. Enjoy a slow crawl down and back, or just float unmoored for a bit.

After you drag yourself out of the pool, you might recover at a poolside table by watching the ball game on TV a while. It occurs to you that this is what the Roman baths must have been like—minus the TV, the background music, and the peach-colored towels.

Onward! Enter a room with four grades of waterfall thundering down from above. Take up a position under one and let the water pound over you—on the top of your head, on your shoulder, over your back. It's like being pitched over Kegon Falls in Nikko (330 feet high, twice Niagara). With the roar of the falls still in your ears, leave to pad through two basins of smooth round stones—first large black ones, then smaller white ones—to waken the bottoms of your feet.

Then soak—s-o-a-k—in the hot water of one of the two generous soaking tubs, one of them furious with jacuzzi. There is no resisting the heat—your muscles surrender and become as noodles. You will find that it is all you can do to haul yourself out to the last room, the room of the softly falling rain.

Now sit down on a little stool and wash yourself. Shave, shampoo, rinse yourself off, then stagger back for one last dip in the all-encompassing holy hotness.

Outfit yourself with a pair of boxer shorts and a peach-colored terrycloth robe and proceed to the Primp Room. Here, in front of a boudoir mirror, you can sit and play with an array of skin creams and aftershave lotions, hair oil, and pomades. There are sterilized combs and hair brushes and blow dryers and toothbrushes and Q-tips to clean your ears.

Now rejuvenated and sleek, adjourn to the snack bar to await your call to the Massage Room. Perhaps a summer salad? A bowl of *oden* stew? Certainly a ¥400 mug of icy draft beer! One gathers that some come to Finlando Sauna every day to soak, eat their evening meal, then curl up on chaise lounges for the night, like peach-colored whales. It is, after all, the cheapest accommodation in town.

In time, your masseuse will come to get you, to lead you to the Massage Room, to stretch you out on the dissecting table. The massage is blissful, far better than the average. There is a teacher of massage in residence, that's why. The masseuses have their meals in their own cafeteria and are supplied with free tickets to any movie showing in Kabuki-cho. The atmosphere in the Massage Room is playful and the masseuses keep up a steady banter among themselves and with any customers who are still conscious.

Afterward, if you want to spend the night (the times of the last trains are posted so you'll know if you have dawdled too long), just tell your masseuse, who will show you to a couch. They may even tuck you in. In my experience, dreams are sweet.

Finlando Sauna (in the basement of the Joypak Building, Kabuki-cho Koma-mae, tel: 3232-8310) is for men only, but there is a good (though not as crazily elaborate) sauna for women in the immediate vicinity:

Green Plaza Ladies' Sauna (1-29-3 Kabuki-cho, tel: 3207-4921) charges ¥2,700 for a sauna from 6 a.m. to 10 p.m., ¥3,300 for a sauna from 10 p.m. to 6 a.m. A massage is ¥3,260 extra.

Tokyo's Public Baths

In the days when few dwellings had their own baths, practically everyone performed their daily ablutions at a sento, *a public bathhouse. These days new apartments, no matter how small, have built-in baths so the public baths are no longer the center of the community they once were. The number of these characterful old places is dwindling as their proprietors reach a certain age and their offspring decline to enter a patently old-fashioned business when all they have to do to make a million dollars is sell the land the old bathhouse stands on. Many people find this situation poignant, as the solidarity of a community that bathes together is a wonderful thing to see.*

Still, there remain over 1,300 sento in Tokyo, mostly in the older neighborhoods. The admission fee and all the hot water you could possibly use is ¥385, an amount set by the city government.

The drill is simple. Enter the vestibule, stow your shoes in a locker, slide open the door appropriate to your sex, and pay the entrance fee to the person sitting behind a raised desk affording a view into both the men's and women's baths. If you require one of the skimpy towelwashcloths known as a tenugui, *or some soap, or a little vial of shampoo, or even a disposable razor, you can buy them too. (In this way, as you wander around the city, when it occurs to you that it might be relaxing to take a bath—just as in other cities you might decide to take a break with a cup of cappuccino at a sidewalk cafe—all you have to do is seek out the nearest* sento, *which is easy as it will have the tallest chimney in the neighborhood.) There can't be many cities where so casual an entrance into the intimacies of community life is possible.*

Take off your clothes and stash them in a locker or a handy basket, enter the tiled bathroom, pull a low stool up to a pair of spigots (one for hot water, one for cold), soap yourself all over, carefully rinse off all of the soap, then ease yourself into the big communal bath where a number of people will be already stewing. The wave of relaxation that overcomes you immediately probably has something to do with the Japanese having the world's highest longevity.

Each sento *has a character all its own. One in Asakusa is famous for its morning-bathers club and a stage which the histrionically inclined can mount to sing a song or tell a joke. Many* sento *have coin-operated laundries attached and some have saunas. In Chiba, there is a* sento *with a built-in French restaurant.*

Here are some of the more architecturally distinguished old Tokyo sento, *with magnificent ceilings and wonderfully fanciful tiling.*

Sekai-yu, *3-8-31 Takadanobaba (tel: 3371-2409). For an extra ¥1,200 you can take a sauna, then cool off in Sekai-yu's own outdoor pond. In the winter, the pond is heated and you can bathe outside, a glorious experience when it's snowing.*

Daikoku-yu, *32-6 Kotobuki-cho, Senju(tel: 3881-3001). Really a magnificent old place, as unabashedly gorgeous as an old-time movie palace. It's been on TV, even.*

Akebono-yu, *4-17-1 Asakusa (tel: 3873-6750). The most famous* sento *in Asakusa.*

Shimizu-yu, *3-12-3 Minami Aoyama(tel: 3401-4404). In a modern building, but very traditional inside, with its own garden.*

Although of no particular architectural interest, you might also like to keep in mind **Koshi no yu**, *1-5 Azabu Juban (tel: 3401-8324), which is one of the city's few natural hot-spring baths. On the third floor of the same building is* **Azabu Juban Onsen** *(tel: 3404-2610, entrance fee ¥ 1,260), which has a sauna, pool, and a large tatami room for sleeping it off. Sushi and bowls of* soba *noodles are for sale. Some people stay all day.*

Akihabara: Belly of the Beast   17

In lower Manhattan, where the International Trade Center's twin towers now stand, there used to be a neighborhood of shops selling all manner of electronic parts and equipment. In every city from London to Lima there used to be some such area, dim, battered, and perpetually in transition, where electronic freaks could go to discuss circuitry and pick up a part or two.

They're all gone now, run over by the furious engine of Tokyo's Akihabara with its hundreds of shops of all sizes: some, six-story buildings staffed by a platoon of uniformed sales people; others, no larger than a closet, with an extraordinarily well-informed proprietor perched on a wobbly stool behind a stack of trays of carefully arranged transistors. Akihabara is the bedrock of Japan's transcendent electronics industry, and it's just two stops past Tokyo Station on the Yamanote Line.

The place spills over with raw commercial energy and off-the-rails electronic wizardry. It is gaudy and jarring, exhausting and exhilarating. It is the world's most high-powered bazaar, with everything always on sale, from voltmeters and logic analyzers to miniature washing machines for miniature apartments, from fiendishly complex

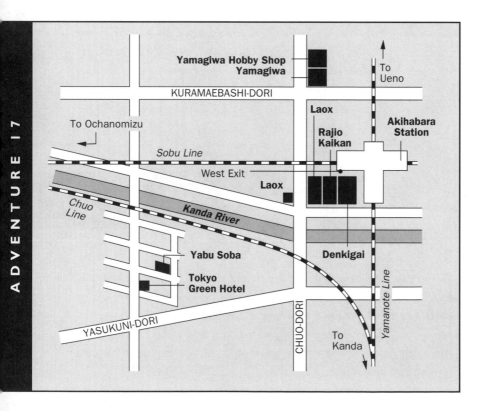

computer games for which there is no export market and domesticated, tea-serving robots to solar-powered ice cream makers and pogo sticks with a battery-powered digital readout of time hopped.

In an area of several city blocks, Akihabara sells 10 percent of all the electronic goods sold in Japan.

Lots of people go to Akihabara as they would go to a circus or a game arcade, just to be energized by the scene, with no thought of making a purchase. Others go with the idea of buying and lugging home an electronic requisite. Their general strategy is to zero in on a model which has just been superseded (the new model will come in a wider range of colors and the knobs will be a different shape) then go from shop to shop angling for the lowest price. (A line drawn through the price posted means haggling is encouraged.)

Visitors from abroad are unlikely to be impressed by Akihabara's prices, though, which may well be higher than at home, even without tax. What attracts is Akihabara's madcap profusion of products of all imaginable categories.

Even before you emerge from the West Exit of Akihabara Station you will be assaulted by promotional hoopla—the passage is lined with show windows full of the spot-lit gadgets of the moment. Just outside the station, in a plaza filled with people scurrying in all directions, you may pause to wonder at a chorus line of chanting cheerleaders celebrating the attractions of a new line of video cassettes— "Super Excellent XDX: XDX we love you!"

A moment's glance will tell you that there is too much here for rational examination. To plod through Akihabara with guidebook in hand would be like touring the universe by referring to a map sketched on the back of an envelope. It's better just to flow with it, to wander, to allow yourself to be pulled along by sounds and signs and curiosities.

Here are some of the things you might run across:

Rajio Kaikan, hacker's paradise. Here is where it all began. Soon after the Great Pacific War ended, a street market in spare radio parts established itself on this spot and grew in such an undisciplined way that eventually it became clear that it would have to be housed. In the early fifties all the little one-man businesses were encouraged to move into Rajio Kaikan ("Radio Building"), now a crumbling Casbah of shops with an absolute minimum of headroom specializing in the stuff of radio mania.

This is where Japan's electronics buffs come to stand enraptured before display after display of trimmers, capacitors, diodes, switches, plugs, and circuit boards, all laid out like jewels. You can buy rare vacuum tubes in their original boxes, which are a bit worn as they have been opened, their contents admired and reverently closed again a thousand times over the 20 years that have passed since the company that made them left the business.

If you can't find what you want at one stand, someone will be happy to direct you to where you can find what you want, no matter how esoteric the part might be. Everything's here, tucked away somewhere. Circuit designers employed by Japan's most sophisticated electronics firms regularly visit Rajio Kaikan just to keep abreast of what's new in integrated circuits, and there is a messenger service (whose minions keep in touch with the home office by walkie-talkies) whose business it is to come here to fill special orders for designers in faraway Nagoya and Osaka.

On the second floor of Rajio Kaikan you can buy antique used equipment like the first portable video tape recorder—a classic, you will be told—for two-thirds off the original price. Only real connoisseurs buy equipment five and ten years old. They like to tinker with it and they are convinced that the first model of any new product is always more solidly built than anything that follows.

Yamagiwa, electronics supermarket. Just up the street from Rajio Kaikan is Yamagiwa. Of Akihabara's two dozen big stores which sell the whole range of electronic products from electric razors to garbage compactors to public-address systems to ultra-sophisticated audio equipment, Yamagiwa is the best staffed and the best organized, and there is somewhat less bustle here than at Laox, its closest competitor.

On Yamagiwa's first floor you will find all kinds of everyday electronics from all manufacturers, like the latest Walkmans and pocket radios as thin as credit cards. On the second floor are hundreds of lamps, hanging from everywhere like golden bats —Yamagiwa started as a lamp store. The third floor is household appliances, like fans and refrigerators.

The fourth floor is for the latest audio and video equipment. There is a sit-down video theater and Akihabara's best existing audio room, where you can sit in a comfortable chair and listen to the pipe organ as reproduced through an Accuphase CD player, a 200-watt Krell amplifier for each of the stereo channels, and two five-foot-tall Apogee "Scintilla" speakers (state-of-the-art American equipment). There used to be a number of rooms like this in Akihabara—better places to listen to music than most concert halls—but recently most stores have felt the need to make the space available for computers and their peripherals, a craze that rages like a forest fire out of control. On Yamagiwa's fifth floor you will find discounted audio and video equipment and on the sixth compact discs and tapes.

Manufacturers like Sony and Matsushita send new employees to Yamagiwa to work as retail clerks on the floor for a month or two to put them in touch with the cruel realities of the marketplace. They keep diaries of consumer reactions during this period and these diaries are closely studied by their company's design engineers and marketing experts for clues to consumer preferences. New products often appear at Yamagiwa a month before they are formally introduced to the market so they can be modified if the reaction of Yamagiwa's discriminating customers is less enthusiastic than expected.

Next door is the **Yamagiwa Hobby Shop**. This might be a good place to buy a memento of the Akihabara scene: a truck which with a few deft manipulations can be turned into a dinosaur; a minicomputer-driven tracked vehicle which, when placed on a large piece of paper, will inscribe intricate designs in many colors; or perhaps an imperious little robot, "Gustav, Storm of Zoids." Most of this stuff is too weird for export.

Dynamic Audio, specialist in used equipment. On the second floor is the maintenance shop where used McIntosh ML275 amplifiers and other items they pick up in the States are brought in for complete reconditioning which includes rechroming the knobs. "Audio maniacs" (the Japanese phrase) come here to buy "dream equipment" (another Japanese phrase) as an investment, at up to 70 percent off the original price, just as those in pursuit of another kind of material perfection might buy a Bugatti.

Laox, headquarters of the largest operation in Akihabara. Laox has half a dozen stores in Akihabara, and can even offer customers use of its own parking garage.

The fifth floor of Laox's main store features a 30-foot wall of a hundred different amplifiers with facilities for comparing their sound, and three separate rooms to listen to speakers. One room has 75 speakers of the type you and I might buy and the other rooms contain the rarefied types for which there may be only a couple of well-heeled customers a year, worldwide.

The floor for personal computers is laid out well and computer fanatics come from all over the city to crack codes, calculate where the comet will hit, and test systems to break the bank at Monte Carlo. The flickering monitors and beep beep bop beep bop of this floor are plainly addictive.

Laox Music, everything for the electronic orchestra. The first floor of the Laox Music building is devoted to electronic keyboards; some, like the Juno 106S Programmable Polyphonic Synthesizer, are almost as complex as the controls of a space shuttle. Mad composers of space music come here to compose reverberations, to push and pull buttons labeled "Wave Aura" and "Wind through the Trees." Manufacturers' representatives are prepared to give you a detailed demonstration—they'll spend hours with you if you like—and when there's nothing particular going on they are apt to stage an impromptu electronic jam session. Upstairs, sets of digital drums and other implements of the New Age.

When you have had enough of dayglo pink, orange, yellow, and green, enough of synthesized music from all directions, enough of sweet entreaties from perky young sales clerks in fishnet stockings and baseball caps, enough of dodging bicycles, enough of distractions and inventions, enough of people in a mass, it is time to break for lunch.

Yabu Soba is the most famous *soba* noodle shop in all of Tokyo and it's only a ten minute walk from where you stand. There may be a line, but it moves fast because Yabu is very efficient. There is a carefully worked-out English menu, and it is difficult to spend more than ¥2,000 for a nourishing meal.

Kyotei Hydroplane Races 18

It is common for foreigners in Tokyo to feel isolated. They wonder, can all this politeness be genuine?

So the intrepid foreigner sets out on a quest to find the *real* Tokyo, that secret place where Tokyoites abandon all affectation and become themselves. The quest leads the traveler first to the Ginza, which is almost as Guccified as Fifth Avenue, then to Asakusa, where the Old Tokyo has been somewhat institutionalized (the better to sell it). In the end, many foreigners become resigned that they will never be privy to what goes on behind the veneer, and they make an uneasy peace with the city: the devil with it.

Before you become similarly resigned, you might like to spend a day at *kyotei*, the hydroplane races. At *kyotei* there is not the slightest tincture of pretense and nobody will pay any attention to you at all as a foreigner. At *kyotei*, Tokyo neglects to shave, hangs a cigarette out of the side of its mouth, puts its feet on the table, and snaps its braces.

There are three *kyotei* courses in Tokyo: Tamagawa, Heiwajima, and Edogawa. Of these, Edogawa is the sportiest venue. Edogawa holds its races two kilometers up the Naka River from Tokyo Bay, where racers must contend with the tide, the current in the river, and the crosswinds off the bay. Edogawa is so tricky that many of the 1,550 professional hydroplane racers in the country (10 percent of whom are female) won't race here at all.

The top *kyotei* racer at the moment is a man named Hikosata, who is 47 years old and weights just 47 kilos. Last year he made ¥100,000,000. The *average* yearly take of a *kyotei* racer is ¥16,500,000 which at ¥130 to the dollar is almost $127,000. In order to qualify as a racer, you must attend training school for a year at your own expense at Motsuko Lake near Mt. Fuji, where you will be taught boat handling, race tactics, and engine mechanics as well as calligraphy and tea ceremony. The school is run along strict military lines.

Racers arrive a day before the race series begins, draw their boats and engines by lot, and spend the day and night practicing and tuning their rigs. The racers must do all their own maintenance, but they are advised and supervised by 16 professional hydroplane mechanics who periodically check the boats to ensure that they are not being surreptitiously souped up. Waxing the bottom is not permitted, for example.

Races are held about 15 days each month. Check the pages of *Nikkan Sports* or call 3656-6111 to make sure the races are on, then take the Sobu Line (from Shinjuku, Shinagawa, Shinbashi, or Tokyo) toward Tsudanuma. After emerging from the long tunnel which runs from Shinbashi to Bakurocho, the train will be on the other side of the Sumida River in a relatively new part of the city. The roads are straighter and wider, the apartment blocks as big as battleships, and the love hotels more overblown.

Disembark at Shinkoiwa (a stop for both express and local trains), exit the station to the right and wait at Stand 2 for a #21 bus which comes along every seven to eight minutes. The fare is ¥160 to Higashi Komatsugawa Shogako-mae, the eighth stop, and the *kyotei* stadium is off to the right (about a 5-minute walk). Just follow the *kyotei* fans studying their tipsheets as they make their way to the stadium.

On an average day, 10,000 *aficionados* pay ¥50 to enter the stadium. Although Edogawa is the smallest of Japan's 24 *kyotei* stadiums, it's the sixth in revenues, bringing in over ¥80 billion in wagers a year. By law, 75 percent of this must be returned to the bettors. After deducting expenses, the stadium turns over the remaining 15 percent to the local government, which in effect runs the operation.

Like *keiba* (horse racing) and *keirin* (bicycle racing), *kyotei* is government-authorized and controlled. The mob has no part in it.

The stadium opens at 10 a.m. (11 on Sundays), with the first race an hour later. There are between 10 and 12 races a day, one every 30 minutes, with the betting windows for the next race open as soon as the preceding race is over.

Before and during the races everybody takes advantage of the stadium's subsidized cafeteria (just like Las Vegas) to down *nikomi* (slices of all parts of pig on a skewer, at ¥70 a skewer), *oden* at ¥70 a selection, and fried croquettes of *aji* fish at ¥100 a plate. Everybody eats standing up at long tables, washing the cheapest food in the city down with cups of tea poured from huge tin kettles, their tipsheets spread out before them.

The crowd is a perfect cross-section of the city. Cunning grandmothers with a system, bumpkins at ease, young couples, studious types who continuously scan the digital tote boards and place their ¥200, ¥500, and ¥1,000 bets (the first two places in any order on the first half of the card; the first two in finishing order on the last half of the card) at the last possible moment, the better to play the odds.

You can watch the races outside from anywhere in the stadium, even on the roof, or inside on a huge TV display.

First, the racers will roar by the stands one by one and their times will be announced, allowing the bettors to adjust their bets on last-minute hunches. The betting windows close five minutes before the start and the *yosoya*, the gravel-voiced tipsters who operate from stalls under signs like "Data company" and "*Kane-chan*" (Old Moneybags), must now post their predictions for inspection by all. Gamblers who have profited by a *yosoya*'s tip will usually slip him a ¥1,000 *pourboire*. This is a gentlemanly sport.

Three minutes before the start, the racers move their boats out onto the course and drift, waiting for the countdown on the big clock at the starting line which is visible to everyone in the stadium. The boats are three meters long and beautifully crafted of wood. The aluminum engines are made to order for these boats by a company that does nothing else, and generate 32 horsepower at 6,600 rpm. They can hit 80 kph on the 300-meter backstretch of the course—that's the speed limit for a small car on a Japanese expressway. After a single season's use, the boats and engines are sold off cheaply and new ones brought in.

Seventy-five seconds before the start, the big clock on the starting line starts to run and the boats jockey for position. The white hand goes around once in 60 seconds, then the yellow hand ticks down 15 seconds to START.

A good start is absolutely crucial. The start is flying, from 80 meters away, and the racers try to be as close to the line as possible with the throttle wide-open when the yellow hand hits the top of the dial. If a racer hits the line before the start, he or she is fined, must go back to school for three days and cannot race for a month, so racers would much rather lose than overshoot the start. But if they are too cautious, they will never win. The start requires very fine calculation, taking into account many factors—even, some insist, the temperature of the water.

The hydroplane on the inside lane has an advantage and will try to exploit it. It's OK to slam into the side of another boat to force it out of a favorable line, but you cannot ram another boat or cut it off. The direction and strength of the wind, the balance of the boat, the racer's skill in jockeying the throttle and timing the corners, the weight of the racer, the tuning of the engine, experience, guts, and sheer luck are the deciding factors.

Some boats throttle back slightly at the first mark to cut it short while others go wide at full throttle, putting a great strain on the thin aluminum fin on the bottom of the boat, which sometimes snaps off. Coming out of the turn, the boats leap out of the water and slam back thwack thwack thwack as they pound down the stretch. The racers wear life jackets, helmets with faceguards, and protective padding on their throttle arms.

By the time the boats have roared around the first mark, position has been established and it is difficult to come through the wash of the leader, especially if he has managed to bully his way to the pole position, thus forcing other boats to swing out and around. The race is three times around the 600-meter circuit, but most of the time it will have been decided by a precision start and a spirited rounding of the first mark.

It's fun to wander around the stadium between races. The tipsters are cajoling the crowd, "This is it folks. This is *your* race. Gather 'round, gather 'round. I'm going to show you what's going to happen," and they move cut-out boats on a board around the first mark to illustrate the likely outcome. In the restrooms, TV monitors show the course so nobody ever has to miss anything, and punters continue to scan their tipsheets even while relieving themselves.

On the roof, weary sportsmen stretch out on benches between races, shoes off, tipsheets over their eyes against the sun. By now the floor is cluttered with betting slips gone wrong and scavengers can't resist inspecting them to see if any have been discarded by mistake. Altogether, *kyotei* is a scene worthy of Breughel and offers about the cheapest entertainment in town. It is the people's circus.

After the last race, board one of the free buses to Hirai, the station on the Sobu Line just before the one you got off coming here. Your fellow passengers, if they are not brooding in silence, will be engaged in an intricate analysis of the day's events, with much gesturing to indicate the position of boats at critical junctions.

Cherry-Blossom Viewing in Ueno Park 19

Winter does not ravage Tokyo, but as the city disdains central heating it must still keep warm by huddling close to kerosene heaters, burrowing under *kotatsu* and quitting warm and companionable offices at the last possible moment. By December, it is dark at breakfast time and dark again by the time the afternoon papers hit the kiosks. By January, a Scandinavian sort of gloom has descended.

Then in mid-February come the first signs of impending release. A shopping street decorates its telephone poles with sprays of plastic flowers, idiot color against a gray city. Subway posters begin to advertise banquet halls for spring weddings by depicting smiling beauties in kimono against a panoply of cherry blossoms. The blossoms seem unreal, a figment of the advertising imagination, but they strike a chord. People loosen their scarves and crack open the window on the train a cautious centimeter.

Sometime in mid-March comes the news that the cherry blossoms, or *sakura*, are blooming in Kyushu. Every night from then on the TV news flashes a map delineating the advancing front. The newspapers take up the theme—in Tokyo the blossoms are *sanbu zaki* (30 percent open), then *gobu zaki* (50 percent open), then *shichibu zaki* (70 percent). Give or take a few days, the blossoms in Tokyo should be *mankai*, in full bloom, sometime in the first week of April.

The city begins to organize for a series of flower-viewing parties called *ohanami*, a pagan celebration of the once-a-year explosion of nature which is all the more glorious because it is so fleeting. (The blossoms are at their peak for three days at most.) The blossoming of the cherry is the natural beginning of the Japanese year. It is when the schools and universities begin the new academic year. It is when the new employees join their companies. It is when everything begins again.

Ueno Park is the most famous place in Japan to view the blossoming cherry. Not the loveliest, not the most horticulturally remarkable, nor the most evocative, and certainly not the most tranquil—just the most famous. To attend *hanami* in Ueno is to watch Tokyo celebrating its Japanese tradition. It is like America at a ball game, Spain at a bullfight, youth at a rock festival. The feeling is: this is who we are—Viewers of Blossoms! Drinkers of Saké! Zingers of Zongs! We are all out of our minds! Yaaaao!

On each of the days the trees are in bloom, a quarter of a million people might wander through Ueno Park. The park is one of Tokyo's largest, accommodating two national museums, a zoo, and a concert hall. But as everyone congregates under the trees in one small section of the park, the scene is Woodstockian. People wander, looking for their party among hundreds of parties, which after a time blur into one great party.

Local companies have strung up hundreds of red lanterns on which their names are conspicuously inscribed, to illuminate the trees. There are parties of ten and twenty, interspersed with larger groups of forty or more. They sprawl (men) or sit primly (women) on flattened cardboard cartons around stacked cases of beer and barrels of saké, their territory delineated by a border of shoes. They feast on platters of sushi, ears of roast corn, skewers of *yakitori*, bananas, pizza, cotton candy, cucumber sandwiches, Champagne, noodles.

There is rhythmic clapping to wobbly singing. Latin music, German folk songs, Russian revolutionary ballads, *enka, chansons,* teenage lullabies and the thunder of ancient drums. Someone starts singing through a bullhorn, his voice cracking. Applause breaks out here, then over there. Like summer lightning, flashes illuminate the scene as people take pictures. One group has lugged in a full-fledged sound system, but even they make no dent in the din.

A large group raises plastic cups in unison to a *"Kanpai!"* Someone in a smaller, very cohesive group leads an elaborate, well-rehearsed cheer. A salaryman in vested suit and striped tie does a wild barefoot dance, then collapses giggling. He is cheered by his group, all business colleagues. An *isshobin* (two-quart bottle) of saké is passed down the line. It gurgles as it is upended. Someone sings solemnly from a song book.

Lovers stroll, people-watching, and feeding each other *yakitori*. A photographer waltzes with his tripod, a man in love with his art. A fanatic sits sipping saké and watching the ball game on a full-sized television set.

It is a genial crowd. The police are headquartered in a great white tent. The chief of the division, gold braid on his sleeve, oversees the carnival like a benevolent *daimyo*. The sweet voice of a policewoman is super-amplified over the hubbub: "Be wary of anyone in your group you don't know. Watch out for your handbags and wallet." A vagrant in his winter regalia of a long tattered topcoat and yachting cap beams a wispy smile at the foreign lady tourist. "I love you," he says. A wandering minstrel in baggy trousers offers to entertain with his *shamisen*, but there are no takers.

Great-grandmothers on the arms of indulgent relatives are brought to see the spectacle. Children come and are indulged with balloons, lollipops, goldfish, and battery-driven pandas. A space is cleared and three mouth organs and a castanet give out with songs of the thirties. Several couples foxtrot on a ballroom floor of flattened cartons and spectators sing along *sotto voce*. A scene from an old movie.

Toward the conclusion of the evening the petals begin to flutter down. It is the beginning of the end for this year. Tomorrow if there is a breeze we will see *hanafubuki*, a storm of flower petals, and the pavement will turn white as with snow.

20   Retro Tokyo

Young Tokyo's vision of the West is colored like a cheap religious oleograph, shot through with tongue-in-cheek romantics, and awash with camp. Young Tokyo is just as fascinated by *Casablanca* as Young Cambridge, Mass., where the Brattle Theater has run this maudlin masterpiece during Harvard exam periods for the past 30 years—the difference being that Young Tokyo is prepared to embrace a foreign style like femme fatale or master spy or punk hot-rodder absolutely without embarrassment because nobody here would be so impolite as to accuse anyone of affectation. Affectation in fact is the whole point—the pop artifacts of the West are in Tokyo simply the trappings for a Beaux Arts costume party.

To cater to this impulse to masquerade, a network of shops has sprung up, mostly in Shibuya. There's Lloyd's Clothing, where it is possible to outfit yourself like Bertie Wooster in spats, a bowler, and a monocle. There's a store called French Surplus where you can buy the uniform of an officer of the Foreign Legion, complete with badges, and get yourself up as Beau Geste. There are lots of places to buy a long silk scarf, a leather helmet, and a pair of antique goggles so you can play at being the intrepid pilot of a Fokker biplane as you clatter around town on your vintage Norton.

By far the most powerful set of images, though, emanates from those golden years of the American Fifties, when there were no personal computers, no acid rain, and no trade friction. Betty Grable! James Dean! Marilyn Monroe! Coca Cola! Harley Davidson! Bobby sox! Juke boxes! Letter sweaters! Fuzzy dice hanging from the rearview mirror of a '56 Chevy!

Leaving this city without having a gander at Retro Tokyo is like bypassing Disneyland on a visit to L.A.

Exit Shibuya Station and walk up Meiji-Dori toward Harajuku.

Okidoki is on the street going off to the right immediately after the pedestrian overpass. There's a '48 Wurlitzer stereophonic jukebox in the window, should you happen to be looking for one and have ¥980,000 to spare. Plastic lawn flamingos if you're lucky enough to have a lawn in this city. Racks of Hawaiian shirts, some fashioned from the silk linings of antique kimono—"Tootsy Wootsy" say the labels. Hula-girl lamps. Key rings. Pocket knives. Chromium bar stools. Hopalong Cassidy lunch boxes. Police badges. Beach towel souvenirs of Florida. In Tokyo, this is exotic stuff.

Continue down Meiji-Dori. "Cat Street," so called because there used to be a lot of cats around here, goes off to the right. There's **Pink Dragon**, one of the founders of the retro scene, looking like an Odeon-Rialto-Metro-Golden picture palace. Pink Dragon sells chaise lounges covered with plastic leopard skin, old Philco TVs, wide neckties hand-painted with palm trees as worn by hard-boiled private dicks, and all manner of nostalgic artifacts carrying the house labels "Cream Soda," "Garage Paradise," and "Hysteric Glamour." The sales clerks at Pink Dragon have slicked-back pompadours that overhang their foreheads by a good three fingers and they sway constantly, snapping their fingers, to songs whose titles are the names of girls.

Other shops in this area are **Town Spot**, with its neon cowgirl sign swinging her leg just like a sign in front of a Las Vegas casino, **Slapshot**, which is the place to buy your Texas Tech "Red Raiders" baseball caps, and **Draper's Bench** and **United Arrows** for cuff links, braces, cricket caps, and blazers.

Take a right at Omotesando and turn left into the first alley. Now you're smack in the middle of Tokyo's thickest gathering of retro shops, with names like **Yanks, Real American Vintage, Shout** ("Twistin' Brothers"), and **Champ** ("Always Delightful Surprise"). There's a billiard parlor, a surf shop, and **Chiao Bambina** and **Mannish**, stylists of modish locks.

A hundred meters down on the left you'll see a Coke-bottle sign as tall as a man. That's **Propeller**, the most magnificent retro store of all.

In Propeller's courtyard there is a brace of perfectly restored, Columbia balloon-tired bikes and, at ¥18,000 a throw, a cluster of the kind of folding chairs U.S. high schools used to use in the auditorium.

The whole place is an attic reeking of nostalgia: old comics and *Life* magazines, cigar humidors, cookie jars, wall clocks advertising Carling's Red Cap Ale and Narragansett Beer, push scooters, Rosebud sleds, park benches from Peoria, music stands, hat racks, tools used by lumberjacks to fell great forests in the days before the buzz saw (for people in a Paul Bunyan mood), sand shovels and pails, Waring blenders, school desks with initials carved, antique air conditioners and fans, Coke machines geared to a nickel, metal signs advertising Mail Pouch Tobacco and Tootsie Rolls and Triple AAA Root Beer which had been nailed to some barn in the American outback before finding their way here, old boxing gloves and older sets of skis, knuckle-busting high school rings, hobby horses, deck chairs from a trans-Atlantic liner, Navajo blankets, a wooden barber pole, a basket of wooden clothes pins, leather flight jackets, a canoe, a cabinet of old telephones, string hammocks, galvanized pails and wash tubs, and a Mobilgas pump cranked by hand. The detritus of America assembled here and laid out for inspection in Harajuku. What does it all mean? I can imagine you are by now reeling from an overload of Betty Boop. Can I suggest a quiet lunch a couple of alleys over in a traditional Japanese restaurant called **Kiku**, which means "Chrysanthemum"? A bowl of noodles and some pickles and tea will cost around ¥1,000. You can rest your bedazzled eyes on the little garden.

I hope I won't disillusion you if I tell you that Kiku is part of the Pink Dragon organization.

Matsuri: **Giving God a Little Jostle** 21

The word is being spread that Tokyo is a city of work soddened drudges so exhausted by their labors that they regularly sleep through their stops on the long commute home. Well, yes, there's something in this.

You will see a very different side of the Tokyoite character though, should you pay a visit to any of the thousands of neighborhood festivals that take place in Tokyo throughout the year. This city is festival *crazy,* to a degree that makes the once-a-year blowouts of New Orleans and Rio seem merely a community-sanctioned occasion to let off a little steam. Festivals in Tokyo are a way of life.

Tokyo festivals are concentrated in time and space (like most everything else in the city) and take a variety of forms, from the sedate *Obon* dances in July in memory of departed souls, to naked festivals where hundreds of young men in loincloths scramble over each other to gain possession of a totem, to fire-walking festivals and Asakusa's giddy **Samba Festival**, which is held the last Saturday in August. Tens of thousands come to watch the inspirational street dancing of nearly naked samba dancers from Brazil counterpointed by the whacked-out but wooded samba dancing of local samba groups like station masters from the East Japan Railways Samba Club in their white summer uniforms.

In Tokyo, every community celebrates its identity with an annual festival, slowly banging the largest drum it can find to summon surrounding communities. Huge apartment blocks, considering themselves to be vertically arranged communities, hold their festival in the street out front. There will be the music of drums and flutes, the dancing of masked fools, kids angling for goldfish and sucking on icy lollipops and chocolate-dipped bananas, grown-ups gnawing on roasted ears of corn flavored with soy sauce and octopus tentacles fried in batter, and there will be wheels of fortune and ¥100 chances to fire a pop gun and win a teddy bear, and there will be stands where you can buy things like gracefully curved bamboo earwax removers, custom-shaped on the spot, and it is all quite irresistible.

The centerpiece of most local festivals is the *omikoshi* ("portable shrine") parade and this is where you come in. Dress as though you are going jogging.

A few weeks before the festival is scheduled to take place, the *omikoshi*, an incredibly elaborate structure of carved black and red lacquered and gilded wood, with brass fixtures and maybe an intricately worked brass phoenix on top, is put on display for everyone to marvel at. *Omikoshi* are the single largest product of Japanese craftsmanship you are likely to run across. Specialists require a year to make one, at stupendous cost, and the oldest ones are 300 years old. *Omikoshi* are the residence of the local *kami*, the local god. It is felt that once a year, the god in the *omikoshi* should be taken out, bounced up and down a bit (to amuse him), and shown around the neighborhood.

On the morning of the festival a ceremonial rigger comes along to tie the *omikoshi* to a sort of raft which is to be hefted on the shoulders of carriers from the community (and anyone else who would like to join in) so the local god can be jogged through the streets. The rigger is soon joined by virtuoso knot-tiers, all offering varying advice, and all garbed, even though they may have come from far away by sub-way, in the manner prescribed by the organizers of the festival: short *happi* coat, short white shorts, *tabi* and straw sandals, and *hachimaki* headband tied over the brow in a way characteristic of the neighbor-hood to keep sweat out of the eyes. A good number of the partici-pants may not be from the area at all, but will be members of one of Tokyo's dozens of *matsuri* (festival) clubs, changing their uniform as required, just because they love the feel of a lively *matsuri*.

The prime mover of the *omikoshi* is likely to be an old man, ordi-narily slightly bent over but now rejuvenated by the spirit of the *matsuri*. At his signal, the carrying team will lift the *omikoshi* onto their shoulders. There may be a dozen carriers in the case of a modest *omikoshi*, or a hundred in the case of the one-ton battleship *omikoshi* of the older neighborhoods. The *omikoshi* transcribes an uneven tra-jectory until the carriers find their rhythm. They are trying to bob the *omikoshi* up and down while keeping it level, not awkwardly at an angle or from side to side. The *omikoshi* is very heavy and it is not easy to coordinate movement. The shoulders of the experienced carriers are heavily calloused as a kind of badge of honor, and the carriers chant "*washoi washoi*" or "*soya soya*" to help set the rhythm. They are as tightly packed as a rugby scrum, the sweat begins to flow, the straw sandals begin to shred against the concrete roadway: they are dancing and in a kind of trance.

Washoi washoi washoi washoi.

There may be young women in the carrying team, with their hair swept up and secured by *hachimaki*. Their fresh appearance is in con-trast to the demeanor of the men, who after a while begin to look as though they are in combat. The *omikoshi* proceeds in fits and starts, retreating several steps before surging on ahead, as in a wobbly barn dance. The carriers begin to experiment with more complex steps — a heel-and-toe clog or a splay-toed shuffle. A team of reinforcements follows carrying rice balls and saké to keep the energy level up and to replace anyone faltering. Taking a god out for a spin is punishingly hard physical work, a tremendous, very conspicuous expenditure of human power in the name of community. A kid is lifted onto the raft and he blows a whistle in time with the bounces; he rises to his feet and everyone cheers. A gathering crowd follows the *omikoshi* which is clearly the festival's center of action.

Wa-shoi wa-shoi wa-shoi wa-shoi.

Join in. Nestle in between two of the carriers. You'll be welcome. *Wa-shoi wa-shoi.* Voices are getting raspy. Carriers drop out to wrap a bandage around a scuffed toe, put down some saké, then get back in. The riggers who follow carrying wooden hammers in their sashes come in to tighten up the ropes which have been loosened by the bouncing. *WA-SHOI wa-shoi WA-SHOI wa-shoi WA-SHOI wa-shoi*—the women are chanting in the offbeat between the chants of the men. Everybody is together, like a great scraggly half-drunken team of rowers stroking a barge. If you are carrying an *omikoshi* you have a license to be crazy. The joy of crowding together belly to back, back to belly, the joy of being Japanese.

Turns are almost impossible to execute smoothly. The *omikoshi* gropes around corners, feeling its way. For the very large *omikoshi* the city has to raise the electrical wiring in the streets. In the old days some *omikoshi* used to go right into the river, cooling everyone off. Sometimes *omikoshi* might have just accidentally taken out the front of the shop of a merchant who was thought to be mean-spirited.

One of the *happi*-coated warriors is wearing pink sunglasses. You will not be out of place in your jogging gear.

Washoi washoi washoi.

After an hour or two, after the *omikoshi* has been duly bounced throughout the neighborhood, it will be lifted reverently onto a set of black lacquer blocks to rest and the carriers, with cracked voices and tattered footgear, will sit on the curb to slump against lampposts to eat and drink and recover their senses. Most *matsuri* clubs will be back at it again next week. *Omikoshi*-carrying can be addictive.

All *omikoshi* parades are fun, but the **Sanja Matsuri**, held toward the end of May in Asakusa is the largest in the country, with more than 100 *omikoshi*, three of them enormous, plus geisha in kimono and lion dancers. It is an amazing scene, a scene you are perfectly welcome to participate in, just as you would be welcome at a carnival anywhere. In fact, foreigners add a certain spice.

Major Tokyo Street Festivals

Listed below are the big blowouts which will be attended by half a million people or more. On top of this, almost every weekend there will be smaller neighborhood festivals, many with a history going back 500 years.

*Also worth noting are the **Tori-no-Ichi** in November at Hanazono Jinja in the middle of Shinjuku and at Otori Jinja in Senzoku, and the **Boro Ichi** in mid-December in Setagaya. These are street markets more than street festivals because there is no omikoshi parade, but there's nothing like them in their diversity and energy.*

All the English-language daily newspapers as well as the Tokyo Journal have festival correspondents who keep track of events.

*May 5. **Kurayama Matsuri**, Okunitama Jinja, Fuchu. Great drum festival in the western suburbs. Eight omikoshi.*

*May, second week. **Kanda Matsuri**, Kanda Myojin. Seven days in mid-May. The festival builds toward the last day, when everyone goes crazy. Maybe 75 omikoshi. Held odd-numbered years.*

*May, third Thursday through Saturday. **Sanja Matsuri**, Asakusa Jinja. Last day is the wildest, with a good hundred omikoshi, some huge. Get there early on Sunday to see the whole drama. Sanja is the granddaddy of Tokyo festivals, with more of everything.*

*June, on the Sunday closest to June 9th. **Yomatsuri** ("Night Festival"), Torigoe Jinja, Asakusa. Possibly the biggest omikoshi in the country leaves the temple in the morning on the shoulders of 200 bearers and returns in the evening by torchlight.*

*Mid-June. **Sanno Matsuri**, Hie Jinja, Nogizaka. In odd-numbered* *years, an elegant procession which goes around the Imperial Palace and back through the Ginza. Brilliant costumes and well-drilled dancing makes this a* matsuri *to see but not join.*

Mid-August. **Hachiman-gu Matsuri***, Tomioka Hachiman-gu, Fukagawa. This downtown parade of lots of* omikoshi *used to end up in the river but now the same end is achieved by everyone just throwing water on everyone else. This is a particularly good* matsuri *for an outsider to join in as it soon gets so sloppy that nobody cares about decorum at all. Held only every three years to allow the neighborhood to recover, it was last held in 1991.*

PART FOUR   *Time Out*

Newcomers to Tokyo tend to feel overwhelmed by the city's frenetic pace. They see people running to catch a train even though the next one is due in three minutes and they wonder if life is really that short. Eventually, though, they learn how to relax, Tokyo style. The most common venues for relaxing are the bar and the bath. When Tokyoites go abroad, it is the little drinking place and the hot water up to the chin—ahhhhh—that they miss the most. But there are other ways to pass the time, too.

Tokyo's Coziest Cinema: ACT 22

If you find it depressing to scan the movie schedules in the Tokyo newspapers, where every movie listed seems to be either the latest blockbuster from Hollywood or a Japanese gangster film, you will be happy to learn that there is a small coterie of Tokyoites who nurture their interest in well-wrought films by frequenting a wondrous little movie theater in Takadanobaba.

The name of this mini theater is **ACT**. You can call 3208-4733 to inquire about titles and times, but when I am in the mood to watch a movie I just go there. The films are always good, sometimes rare, and often remarkable. Past offerings have been classic French, German, and Italian films, American films like the first movie of Cary Grant and Katherine Hepburn, and fine Japanese films which, because they were not made with an eye to the mass audience, remain unknown except to specialists. A ticket is ¥1,500 for the majority of ACT's double-feature programs, but sometimes a few hundred yen more for films which have been particularly difficult to procure. Because I find the Takadanobaba area wonderful for aimless wandering, I don't plan an ACT day in much detail. I usually make it a habit first to drop in at **Biblos** bookstore near the station to check out the new magazines and paperbacks. Biblos has the best collection of Penguins in town. Then I wander up Waseda-Dori toward Waseda University, browsing in the little used bookstores that line the avenue. (A nice gift to someone who is amused by curiosities would be an old Japanese book of etiquette with illustrated advice on how to conduct oneself at a

Western table. The ritual seems as complex as a coronation. The bookstore nearest ACT seems to specialize in this sort of thing for a few hundred yen.)

On your way, check out what's playing at the old **Waseda Shochiku** movie theater, which is very much like any diehard art-film theater you would find in Philadelphia or Paris—slightly scruffy but comfortable enough if you can find a chair in one piece. The Shochiku (tel: 3200-8968 or 3232-9787) has interesting double features, but they do not have the scope of ACT's programs, as most of the films they show were made within the past five years or so. They are also apt to throw in the occasional stinker *pour épater les bourgeois.* Tickets are ¥1,300 for adults, ¥1,100 for students.

When you finally wend your leisurely way to ACT, if you're like me you'll undoubtedly find the movie began ten minutes earlier. As ACT very sensibly admits no one in midstream, you will have some time on your hands. The thing to do in this case is to adjourn to **Chez Nous** just down the street. Chez Nous is a student coffeehouse with the feel of Vienna. Students come to read whole books or write long letters, and couples come to talk softly for hours at a time, trying to figure each other out. Chez Nous is dim and quiet, with a brick fireplace, lots of reading material and comfortable bentwood chairs. A cup of cappuccino dusted with cinnamon costs ¥480.

Make your way out of Chez Nous a few minutes before the movie is scheduled to begin. There may be a few people lined up on the stairs, but it will be nothing like the crush of humanity you experience in any cinema in Shinjuku. ACT holds only 50.

Pay your ¥1,500. You'll be given a copy of the schedule of coming events and a little questionnaire asking what you thought of the movie. The projector is right there, just behind the young lady selling tickets. Take your shoes off and push them through the slot in the bottom of the ticket desk. You'll be given a wooden counter for them.

Inside the theater there are no chairs, only backrests with a bolster. You sit on the rug on the floor, as you would sit in your living room. The three rows of seats are graduated in height, the better to see. The theater is immaculate, the screen only 15 feet away is the size of a bed

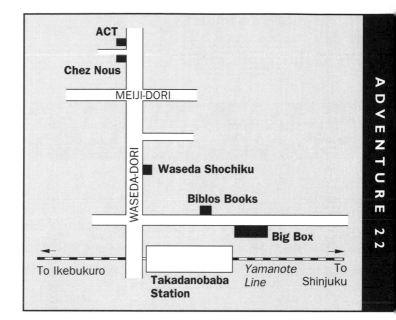

sheet. The audience, film buffs all, read the books they brought with them while waiting for the movie to start.

Finally, the young lady at the counter steps on to the little stage and says a few words about the film, which may be some dreamy Japanese melange of Fellini, Chaplin, and E.A. Poe, or it may be "Battleship Potemkin" teamed up with an early Hitchcock thriller. Seeing it in this little place with a rapt audience, it will be as films used to be—an immediate experience, magical. As the film unwinds you will find yourself slumping back against the bolster so that you are on the floor looking up at the screen, your fingers intertwined behind your neck.

When the movie is over, everyone must retrieve and put on their shoes and studiously fill out their questionnaire, and as the vestibule is only large enough for one person at a time it takes a few minutes for the theater to empty. When you hand in your counter to get your shoes back, you will be given a piece of candy. ACT used to serve free tea and cookies during the intermission, but as they're just slightly caught up in the rush of things these days, they've stopped doing that.

23 Gotenba Onsen

Among this country's most seductive attractions are its hot spring baths. There are several thousand *onsen*, as they are called, scattered about Japan. These islands are still seething with volcanic activity, and while the business may not be growing, it is hardly in a decline.

The classic *onsen* is a poetic vision: one bathes outdoors in a bubbling wellspring of mineral water in a secluded ravine lined with ancient moss and green bamboo, a beaker of the local saké floating on a tray at one's elbow, and across the way, dimly perceived through the mist on the water, your companion gives you a shy smile. The moon comes out from behind the clouds and it begins to snow....

But let us be realistic. The tendency for a caravan of tour buses to pull up just as you are easing yourself into a famous bath is well-established. The really rustic *onsen* require a train journey of several hours, most likely followed by a longish ride on a bus full of fellow pilgrims in the grip of a celebratory mood. Because your pursuit of the classic bath will lure you far away from Tokyo, you must plan to spend the night, which can be expensive even if you find accommodations in the cavernous old barracks, the *onsen*'s most conspicuous lodgings. In the evening, after an elaborate but unremarkable dinner in your room, you can hobble into town wearing *geta* and *yukata* and seek diversion in non-electronic pachinko. As for your coy companion, only recall that friendly mixed bathing was the rule in this country before Western Civilization tramped in with muddy boots. It is painful to realize that our own damn foolishness undid this pleasant custom.

Some people are so confounded by their search for the ideal bath they never find one they can really enjoy. This is extremely unfortunate.

In order that you not fall prey to this sad condition, I am going to tell you about a wonderful *onsen* that is near enough to Tokyo to easily return on the same day, that is very possibly the most congenial *onsen* in the country, because everyone there tends to know each other that has the most spectacular view of any *onsen* because it looks out immediately on Mt. Fuji, and that, because it is not a commercial venture, costs only ¥1,000 for as many soul-satisfying soaks as you feel up to.

Amazingly, the place is not marked on any *onsen* map I have ever run across, which means there are no tour buses!

I refer to **Gotenba Onsen**, the public bath administered by the city of Gotenba, Shizuoka Prefecture, a farming community of about 70,000 nestled right up against the world's most famous mountain. The area, whose softly rolling hills evoke Tuscany, used to be Imperial Hunting Grounds.

The *onsen* was built in 1980 as the centerpiece of the community. For local people it is far more than a place to come to get clean—it is more like a Roman bath must have been. Especially during the winter when chores are not as demanding, Gotenba farmers and their families come to spend the whole day soaking and talking and nibbling and napping. The farmers of Gotenba must be the world's cleanest, as well as maybe the world's most content.

There are three ways to get to the *onsen*. Normally, the most efficient way is by car on the Tomei Expressway. It's about a hundred kilometers from downtown Tokyo to the Gotenba Exit and shouldn't take more than an hour and a quarter if you can go on any day but Sunday and have reasonably good luck. On a fine summer day, however, good luck will be scarce. The toll is ¥2,500. The Tomei will feed you into Route 138, at which point go left toward Hakone, *not* Gotenba City. This will take you up the hill, past two museums devoted to the art of the sports car, past a fantastic white temple on the right and a white windmill on the left. Take the first left after the windmill and go 150 meters down the hill to the white, rather Bauhaus *onsen*. Park in the parking lot or, if that is full, in the street.

Alternately, you can drive right out on Route 246, a more scenic route through the mountains and tea terraces which will take, however, at least an additional hour but cost nothing in tolls.

Still another possibility is the Odakyu Line train from Shinjuku to Matsuda, and change to the Gotenba Line for Gotenba. The train will cost ¥2,920 one way, but then you must take a bus (for ¥330, only one per hour) or a taxi (about ¥1,700) to "Gotenba-shi Onsen Kaikan."

Divest yourself of your fancy city shoes at the entrance and put them in the rack with the no-nonsense footgear of the local folk. Pay your ¥500 to the lady at the front desk, and an additional ¥120 if you want to rent a *yukata*, a light cotton kimono ideal for slipping into between baths. If you haven't brought your own wash towel (called a *tenugui*) and your own soap and shampoo, you can buy them at the front desk.

If you have come in a group of six or more you might consider reserving one of the four small private tatami rooms. They are free and will allow for a more unrestrained party, but in doing so you miss out on the free and easy spirit which prevails in the large communal tatami room, with shoji along two walls opening out onto a balcony which overlooks the city. It's just like joining a huge family sprawled out over four or five generations.

Stake out your area and head for the baths, men to theirs and women to theirs. Ah, the bath. Like returning to the womb, the natural state of innocence. Lightly sulphured water, soft on the skin and good for rheumatism, they say. And lack of perspective, I say. After a time, even the jaw muscles loosen. There is no idle chatter as your fellow bathers are sunk in reverie, gazing out on the mountain. They move lazily, like sleepy porpoises. The only reason to leave this bath is to return, as if by habit, to a distracted world.

But eventually habit prevails and back in the big room, refreshed as though your heart has been massaged, you slump up against one of the long tables that stretch across the room and use your last bit of strength to pry open a can of beer.

People in various stages of undress lounge at the tables and read letters or magazines, or stretch out and doze off, or watch the TV in the corner through half-closed eyes. Everybody eats (*bento* brought from home or the *sashimi* and *oden* brought up from the farmer's cooperative in town and sold at cost—¥400 a portion) and drinks (beer and saké and endless pots of tea), so by mid-afternoon the room is in such a state of comfortable disarray that it looks like a suburban living room after a huge family has finished reading the weekend newspaper.

After a decent interval, return for your second bath, then maybe a session in the mechanical massage chairs which are worth figuring out how to adjust. Their use is free and the experience is addictive.

The day begins to slip away and you notice the sun is going down behind Fuji. Perhaps just one more bath....

Gotenba is open from 10 a.m. to 9 p.m. in the summer and 10 to 7 in the winter, except Mondays. On New Year's Eve it is open from 5 in the afternoon until midnight and on New Year's Day from 5 in the morning until noon. Tel: 0550-83-3303.

Climbing Mt. Ishiwari 24

Eighty percent of Japan is mountainous, and a similar percentage of the population are mountaineers at heart. City dwellers dream of the mountains as a refuge abounding in delicate ferns and sweet berries and great rolling expanses of moss — and innocence and freedom.

So every year, beginning April 1, which is *yamabiraki* or "mountain-opening day," the lemmings leave Tokyo to trudge in a long line, as if on a stalled escalator, slowly, slowly up Mt. Fuji, "The Mountain." The Fuji ascent is an annual rite for masochists, of which this country has more than its share. The climb is tiring, boring, and aesthetically threadbare, although the view from the top is otherworldly, as any view from 3,776 meters must be. Fuji-san, you see, is a spent volcano, an enormous pile of cinders. There is a Japanese proverb which holds that while it may be a reasonably rewarding experience to climb Fuji once, only fools climb it twice.

No, it is far more fulfilling to contemplate Fuji from a congenial vantage point than to conquer it, and I have the perfect vantage point in mind—a jewel of a mountain in the Fuji foothills, with a well-cared-for trail which offers good exercise but does not require undue acrobatics, a modest shrine midway up and fine views. Most miraculous of all, it is never crowded—indeed, there is a good chance that you will have the mountain all to yourself. Mt. Ishiwari ("Mount Split Rock") will be our secret.

It takes about three hours to get to Ishiwari from Shinjuku, by train and by bus. The climb itself, up and down, takes about two hours, if you do not allow yourself to be detained by the spectacular view of Fuji and Lake Yamanaka from Ishiwari's summit. (But it is certain that you will be detained by the view, particularly if you have thought to tuck into your rucksack a good *bento* and a thermos of something refreshing.)

It is perfectly possible to do the climb in tennis shoes, but be assured that at the end of the day you'll be pleasantly wrung out and ripe for a good soak in a hot bath.

At Shinjuku Station, buy a ticket for Fuji Yoshida at the ticket counter next to Track 5 and 6. The train, which leaves every Sunday at 8:11 a.m. from Track 6, is the "Holiday Kaisoku Picnic-go." It arrives at Fuji Yoshida at 10:21 a.m. and the fare is ¥2,270 one way. Call Shinjuku Station Information at 3355-4400 to confirm details. Be sure to take a seat in one of the first three cars.

Most of your traveling companions will be mountain lovers trekking off to hikes better documented by the guide books than is Ishiwari. They will be sporting plus fours, heavy hiking boots with scarlet laces, and soft caps sprinkled with alpine badges. The kids will be packing pastel rucksacks with a Snoopy motif, and they are almost certain to have miniature plastic thermoses dangling by their side.

At Takao, 58 minutes out of Shinjuku, the train is at the western boundary of Tokyo. Soon after, it enters a long tunnel to emerge in a rural landscape of brilliant green fields of rice, well-tended forests, rapids cascading in ravines, and thatched farmhouses in groves of persimmon trees. At Otsuki ("Big Moon") the train stops for a few minutes. When the train starts again, the front three cars (where you should be) separate from the main train and move on to a single track line.

Now there is a station every mile or so and the train takes on the aspect of a trolley. At Mitsutoge, many of your fellow travelers will disembark. Mitsutoge is a certified Famous Mountain with a six-hour climb. Let them go.

Fuji Yoshida at the end of the line is an immaculate station, quite large, as befits the transportation center for the area. Buy a bus ticket for Hirano (¥690); there's a bus about every hour on the hour from Platform 1.

It's a 40-minute ride to Hirano, past many *minshuku* pensions, tennis courts, and country inns, for this whole area is infested with resorts. The bus runs along the shore of Lake Yamanaka with its fleet of swan boats, halfway around the lake to Hirano. Disembark, cross the street and head down the road with the coffee shop called Joy Patio on it. About 500 meters down the road you will spy a small red *torii* gate with a little red-roofed shrine behind it. Turn off here to the left between the two stone pillars inscribed in Japanese *Ishiwari Jinja*—"Ishiwari Shrine." This is the beginning of the path.

After an interlude you will come out on a soccer field. Cross it and enter the woods on the opposite side. Eventually you will come to a *torii* with a sign saying *Ganbare!* which means "Go for it!" On either side of the stairs there are columns inscribed with the names of businesses that have pledged to maintain the path. The steps go practically straight up, as if to suggest that if it isn't work to get there, it isn't worth going. The climb up these steps to a brace of benches is the most strenuous part of the climb and will take about 20 minutes. At the benches you will probably be inclined to take a short break.

When you start off again you'll find you have hit a rhythm. You'll come across three mossy boulders in the middle of the path. The boulders are linked with a length of hemp rope and a pattern of paper, a Shinto gesture. People sometimes leave a few coins on the biggest boulder as a nod to fate; just in case, who knows. In former times, samurai were required to dismount their horses at this point, and this used to be as far as women were allowed to trespass.

After a stretch that you will have to haul yourself up with a conveniently placed series of nylon ropes, the ground will level out and you will emerge at Ishiwari Jinja. It's a simple shrine, not much larger than a tool shed. In front sit a pair of iron *geta*, the shrine's only ornament. Supplicants come to make a wish, perhaps marking their visit with a brush-written note and possibly leaving behind a bottle of saké, for the gods of Shinto are thirsty. Most people who climb Ishiwari are not mountain lovers on a lark, but people seeking help and consolation.

The *jinja* snuggles up to a huge split rock as tall as a two-story building. You can go up behind the rock and walk through the crevice, which is cleaved as clean as cracked ice. Water drips into a bucket concealed in a rift in the rock. It is said that this water is good for eye and skin ailments.

Let's continue on. Be careful here. The sign points the way. The path goes up, not down. Another large rock, surrounded by cairns, then a bit further and you emerge on the bald summit—1,413 meters —and there is Fuji-san smack in front of you. It is like looking up at a magnificent monument 500 times the size of anything the most fanatical of the pharaohs ever dreamed of, and only a lush valley lies between you and it. Break out the *bento*.

To return by a different route, descend in the direction of Fuji. There are stairs, sort of. Only the first 200 meters is rough, then you'll find yourself walking through a field of Japanese flowers of the field— *susuki, noazami, miyakowasure* ("forget-the-city"), *yamahagi, nogiku.* Watch out: at one point there's a switch-back—follow the sign to Hirano. The descent is a stroll compared to the climb—a promenade along a ridge overlooking the lake. You should come out at the first *torii.* If in doubt, just keep heading toward the lake.

Then back to the bus to Fuji-Yoshida, and the train back to Shinjuku, and home and that bath.

Browsing in Jinbocho   25

In Tokyo, everybody reads. A favorite diversion is *tachiyomi*—"standing-reading"—easing a volume off a shelf in a bookstore and devouring it on the spot.

This afternoon I thought we'd wander around the Jinbocho section of Kanda, one of the world's great concentrations of used-book dealers. There are three extraordinary shops which deal in books in English and other European languages which I particularly want to point you toward.

Make your way to Ochanomizu Station on the Chuo Line and take the West Exit. "Water for Tea" is a lovely place name, but there is nothing languid about the plaza in front of the station, which is a popular venue for loudly amplified student protests about the disorderly state of the world.

Note the five-story Sun Royal coffee shop next to the station, with its allegorical stained-glass windows and lumbering Corinthian columns. It's a relic of a time when Tokyo espoused the Disney school of architecture. The influence of this school can still be seen in the design of Tokyo's love hotels, where more or less anything still goes.

Head down Ochanomizu-Dori toward Jinbocho. Ochanomizu-Dori is a street devoted to the distractions of college students, particularly those from Meiji University, whose great brooding hulk of a main building is a few hundred meters down the street on the right. There are cheap eateries, record stores, video stores, computer stores, and stores which discount all manner of sports equipment—a little Akihabara for tennis racquets and mountain-climbing gear. There are three stores crammed with every kind of musical instrument imaginable: one of them has a wall display of 60 mandolins.

Ochanomizu-Dori runs into Yasukuni-Dori at the first big intersection. Most of Jinbocho's 133 bookstores are strung out along the south side of Yasukuni-Dori. The browsing fodder is a serendipidarian's delight, the jetsam remaining from a couple of generations' student years abroad and the abandoned libraries of foreigners who have moved on. Here you will find dusty tomes meticulously annotated in Japanese like *The Dynamic Natural Gas Industry* (University of Oklahoma Press) and *The Problems of Land Transfer* by Karunamoy Mukerji, M.A., Ph.D., bearing a bookseller's sticker from the Oxford Book and Stationery Company, New Delhi.

You might also find, as I once did, a first edition of James Joyce's *Ulysses*, pages uncut, as published in Paris by Shakespeare and Co., for ¥5,000. (A few weeks later I went back to the same shop and found that another copy had been fitted into the same spot on the same shelf.)

Not far off the intersection you will find **Subunso**, founded in 1945, a bookshop which caters to the confirmed bibliophile. Along the wall in the entrance way are stacked sets, like the complete *Nonesuch Dickens* (¥1,300,000) and *Oeuvres Completes* of the Marquis de Sade in eight leather-bound volumes. The walls are hung with framed autographed letters of the likes of Napoleon and Darwin and with engravings of the loci of bibliographical pilgrimages like Duke Humphrey's Library in the Bodleian.

Upstairs at Subunso there's a sturdy section on Japan, where you could pick up the four volumes of R.H. Blyth's commentary on haiku

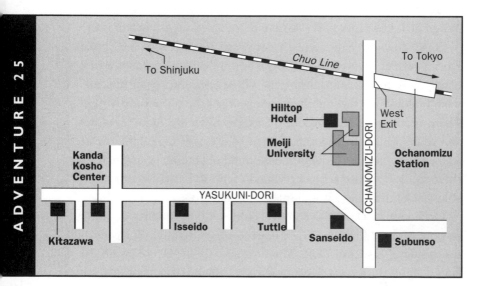

for ¥13,500 or any of the slender volumes of the pre-war Tourist Library that might strike your fancy, perhaps *The Cult of Tea* which, in a series of grim rotogravures, portrays the drinking of that beverage as the most austere of human activities.

Subunso's "Taste, etc." section (so labeled) is full of wonderful odds and ends like *The Mummy* by Wallis Budge, Cambridge U.P., 1925; *Magician's Own Book, 999 Startling Tricks*, Edinburgh, 1871; *Hutchinson on Witchcraft*, London, 1720; *Johnson's Notebook for Tea Planters* ("Dedicated to All Earnest-minded Young Men of the Tea Industry"), Colombo, 1951; and *The History of Underclothes* by C. Willet and Phillis Counnington, London, 1953.

Moving west on Yasukuni-Dori, you'll run into **Nanyodo**, Books for Architects. The building is self-conscious in its role as arbiter of design—it's all concrete and angles. Outside, there are stacks of used copies of *Architectural Record* and *Kenchiku Bunka*.

Sanseido—no used books, only new—is the largest bookstore in Japan. It's always jammed. The fifth floor is for "Overseas Books," a generally uninspired collection mainstayed by the works of Thomas Hardy, Somerset Maugham, and Graham Greene, the perennial favorites of local students of the English novel. On the magazine rack are current copies of *The Times, Le Monde, Frankfurter Allgemeine Zeitung*, and the *International Herald Tribune*.

On down Yasukuni-Dori, past Charles E. Tuttle Company (publishers and booksellers with offices in Tokyo and Boston), past Oya Shobo, which specializes in mathematics and Marxist philosophy with books like *The Heat Equation, Curvature and Homology*, and *Markov Chains* in its tiny window, past Matsumura & Co., which always has outside a scattering of oversized picture books—*The Maori, Historic Houses of Britain, Great Moments in Football*—to the magnificent **Isseido**, whose second floor, reached by a wide marble staircase lined with somber scholarly sets, is a mecca for antiquarian book collectors around the world.

At Isseido you will find things like Soren Kierkegaard's complete works in Danish, *The Works of Ruskin* in 35 volumes, and *Galleries Historiques de Versailles* in 16 leather-bound elephant folios, all displayed confidently, as if a buyer were expected momentarily. Isseido's collection has its biases, as any characterful collection must, being particularly strong in works on typography, mountaineering, railways, bridges, wine, and ornithology. There's a good corner on Japan, with evocative curiosities like *Romances of Old Japan* by Madame Yukio Ozaki, London, 1919, and Engelbert Kaempfer's *Monumental Histoire de l'empire du Japan*, The Hague, 1729, two massive volumes with engravings for ¥480,000—cheap, surely. Isseido's second floor is where I found my copy of *Ulysses*.

Now to clear the head a bit let's take a quick tour of the Kanda Kosho ("Bargaining") Center—nine floors of junk, mostly. Take an elevator to the top floor, which features old foreign and domestic 78s and LPs, and a collection of wind-up phonographs (expensive). The eighth floor is devoted to pornography; the seventh movie stills, posters, and magazines; the sixth caters to collectors of antique postcards, hideous mass-produced prints, stamps, coins and old lottery tickets; the fourth floor is for books about art and old kabuki and noh magazines (¥100 each); the third floor is a rabbit warren of shops with people peering out from behind great stacks of books with no discernible theme except for the shop which specializes in books about birds; the second floor is for comics (classics are kept in glass cases) and the ground floor is an old-book bazaar.

Our last shop is **Kitazawa**, a store for readers as opposed to collectors, and for its size it is perhaps the best bookstore in the world. An elegant place, Kitazawa has a white marble floor, carved mahogany bookcases which reach to the ceiling, and a brass-railed carpeted staircase befitting a country house. Mozart usually tinkles in the background.

The first floor is new books, both hardback and paper, all carefully chosen. There are 14 bookcases of literature: Samuel Pepys, Jay McInerney, Philip Roth, William Blake, and not just the well-known works. Kitazawa puts its own glassine jacket over the cover of every book on its shelves.

Upstairs is the used-book collection, just as carefully chosen—Evelyn Waugh, J.B. Priestley, P.G. Wodehouse, Ford Madox Ford, Max Beerbohm, classic thrillers — a strong injection of Anglophilia. There is a separate room with club chairs for inspection of rare volumes and on the second floor a comfortable couch for browsers weary of *tachi-yomi*. A civilized place. With a bookstore like Kitazawa, no resident of Tokyo need ever yearn for the bookstores of London or New York.

You must be exhausted after all this rummaging around in odd enthusiasms. Dinner at **Balalaika**, an old, established Russian restaurant at Kanda Jinbo-cho 1-63 (tel: 3291-8363) would be restorative and not terribly expensive.

Then back up to Ochanomizu Station and home.

Initiation to Go 26

The best games are those whose rules are simple but whose strategies are complex. By this definition, the ancient game of *go* is the best game ever devised. There are a half dozen very simple, easy-to-understand rules, but the depths of the game are unfathomable. Computers have been programmed to play chess at a world-class level but no one has yet figured out how to program a computer to play *go* beyond a weak amateur stage. *Go* fanatics insist that you have to start playing by the age of eight or you'll never be able to garner the experience necessary to compete with the big boys.

Which is not to say that you can't have fun dabbling in the game. But be wary. *Go* is seductive and, like chess, has the power to draw you into another world. *Go* players look at patterns of tiles in the sidewalk and are reminded of classic positions on the board. It is certainly possible to learn the rudiments and polish your game in New York or London or Amsterdam, cities where the game has many resident devotees, but how much better to be initiated into the delights of *go* in Tokyo, at one of the strongest *go* clubs in Japan.

The **Takadanobaba Igo Club** (tel: 3208-0279) is open every day from noon until 10 p.m. and is located on the seventh floor of the F.I. building, around the corner from The Big Box (see Adventure 22).

When you first come upon the place, it appears to be a gambling den. It's one large, smoke-filled room crammed with tables with *go* boards on them, two chairs to a table. The only sound is the plunking of stones on boards and the occasional grunt as someone is confronted with a flaw in his game. Concentration is so intense the air crackles.

People come from all over the country and even from abroad to play in this room. A number of players are top amateurs, close to professional level. Tables are occupied eight hours a day by students from Waseda University just up the road, who forsake their studies to try to get a handle on this most elusive of all games. At the front desk you can pay ¥1,200 for the day and get yourself assigned an opponent of similar strength. Habitués are ranked as on a tennis ladder.

You'll not want to engage an opponent, though, until you've got some idea of how the game works. As it happens, an American named Jonathan Wood is prepared, on payment of ¥2,000, to give you a lesson in English on Mondays, beginning at 7 p.m. He'll explain the rules and either pit you against another beginner or play you a game himself, pointing out how your play might have been better at critical junctures. Then he'll present you with an elementary text and a chit which will allow you to buy books and magazines at a discount at the fourth floor English-language bookstore called Biblos, which is owned and managed by a *go* fanatic and which stocks the complete line of Penguin paperbacks.

27 Underground Theater

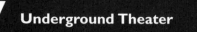

It is an illusion that the only movies playing in Tokyo are Hollywood blockbusters, and that most Tokyo theatrical productions are large-scale renderings in Japanese of faded Broadway musicals. The thing is, it's just that sort of event that gets advertised on six-story-high banners in the Ginza.

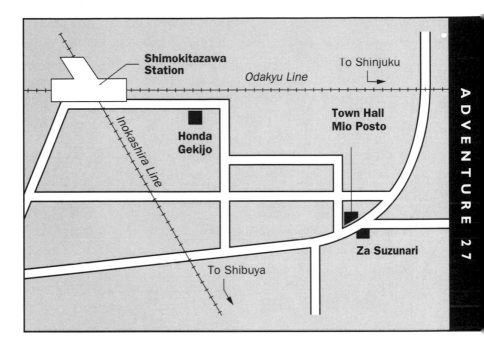

Actually, Tokyo is fermenting with the theatrical activity of maybe 2,000 amateur theater groups. A typical group will have forged its association during college (Waseda University is said to have 30 or so groups hammering away at any given moment), and will have kept together after graduation, adding new members when suitable applicants present themselves. Group members range in age from 25 to about 30 and everyone has another job.

It's all a labor of love, of course. Typically, the group's charismatic leader/playwright/director will write one new play every year or even every six months, with everyone giving suggestions as the script takes form. (A typical plot will examine the possible repercussions of an unannounced appearance of Jesus Christ in a noodle shop in Hokkaido, and what happens in Act Two when He loses his luggage during a sightseeing trip to Tokyo.)

The group will normally meet after work once a week in a park for voice training and wind sprints, and once a month at a favorite coffeehouse, when the director will assign parts and jobs like program editor and poster designer. Posters, the play's single effort at promotion, will be displayed in sympathetic coffeehouses and bars, and in the foyers of little theaters all over town. Members of the group will chip in a few thousand yen each month to maintain a tiny office in a low-rent neighborhood. About ten days before the play opens, members will go into *gasshuku* (sort of an intensive training camp), when they will hire a place where they can run through the whole play two or three times a day while never leaving the building—eating all meals together and then sleeping together in one room after a long day of rehearsals and grueling sessions of self-criticism.

These groups are forging the new Japanese theater, which is socially and politically aware and suffused with a wacky theatricality. Groups such as Dai San Erotica and Tokyo Kid Brothers have performed in the U.S. and in Europe.

The theaters which stage performances by amateur groups are called *shogekijo* ("little theaters"). They are all over town but heaviest on the ground in Shinjuku (where Kinokuniya Hall and Space Den are favored venues—I don't think I'll ever forget watching the chorus line of a home-grown musical kicking up with absolute precision on Space Den's 12-foot-wide stage), in Shibuya (where Tiny Alice across the street from Isetan is very active), and in Ikebukuro, which in Tokyo terms is off-off-Broadway.

Admission is ¥800 to ¥2,500, depending on the respectability of the theater and what the troupe thinks it can draw. There's usually no stage and no curtain; scene changes are made during blackouts. In many little theaters there are no seats either, so the audience sits on cushions on the floor, shoulder to shoulder, knees drawn up in front of them. It is often so crowded that briefcases and shopping bags have to be checked at the door, and the audience is warned that because it can get very warm during the performance, they should divest themselves of their sweaters now as it will be difficult to take them off once everyone gets settled in.

There is a pecking order among *shogekijo*, of course. One of the most respected, because it is one of the oldest and has staged a lot of performances by groups that have gone on to make their mark, is **Za Suzunari** ("The Jam-packed") in Shimokitazawa. Shimokitazawa is a perfect place for alternative theater: it's as close as any part of Tokyo gets to being a college town, with its host of cheap bookstores, jazz coffeehouses, and record stores.

The **Honda Gekijo** at the South Exit of Shimokitazawa Station is the most established of Shimokitazawa's four main theaters. (Za Suzunari spawned the Honda.) You might want to drop in at the Honda Gekijo's box office, which acts as a clearing house for information on what's going on at the local theaters, and ask them what they would recommend for someone whose colloquial Japanese is less than fluent. Basically, you're looking for something *manga-poi*, that is, as broadly acted as a teenager's action comic. In the absence of clues to the contrary, head for Za Suzunari (tel: 3469-0511). Maybe you'll run across something like "DUAL-P: The Romantic Hemoglobin Show," as presented by a group which calls itself the Paranoia Department Store.

After the performance, you might consider dropping in to Mio Posto, a fine little Italian restaurant in the basement of Kitazawa's magnificent new town hall or, if you are in a more casual mood, to Focolare, not far from the station's North Exit, where a seat at the counter puts you in the middle of a lively scene and everything is touched with garlic.

Kichijoji Jazz Joints 28

Thirty years ago, smoky little jazz joints were as thick on the ground in Shinjuku as bamboo shoots in early spring. They were a kind of political statement. The scene is not so intense now, but jazz still resonates deeply in Tokyo's soul. Sleek American jazz houses like Blue Note and Blues Alley have established bridgeheads here and it is generally acknowledged that Japanese jazz has finally managed to wean itself away from American models and begun to forge its own identity.

A visit to **Sometime**, a wonderfully characterful jazz venue where a new generation of Japanese jazz musicians is busy cutting its teeth, can be a joyous occasion. At Shinjuku Station, take the Chuo Line local from Platform 14 to Kichijoji. It's six stops and costs ¥210. The Chuo Line runs through the vastness of the western suburbs and is the axis along which most of Tokyo's future growth is destined to occur. Kichijoji is the Harajuku of the Chuo Line—the focal point of youthful energy for the whole west side of the city. There's nothing very grand here: the idea is cheap chic. Sometime is in a little alley just off Kichijoji's Sun Road, one of Tokyo's most unrestrained shopping malls. Its address is Ishikawa Building, B1F, 1-11-31 Kichijoji-honcho, tel: 0422-21-6336.

Down a set of well-worn stairs to the basement where you'll be welcomed by an attentive young waitress with a hip haircut. The place holds maybe eighty. Table charge is ¥1,000 to ¥1,500, depending on who's up. There is a trio of wooden saloon tables within an outstretched arm of the band, a bar constructed of old bricks with sight lines over the piano player's shoulder, and a couple of cozy back rooms. The walls are brick and sullen, artistically scored concrete.

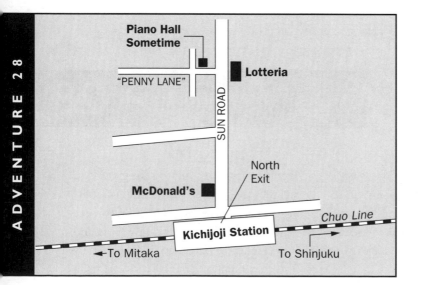

Scattered about with the offhand calculation of a flower arrangement are artifacts—an antique Swedish telephone, some old brass reading lamps with green glass shades, a faded illuminated sign proclaiming "Miller, the Champagne of Beers," an English bus stop sign. The room is held together by gray steel girders joined together by massive bolts. The place looks like the stage set for a New York subway station which an absent-minded set designer has provided with a grandfather clock, a wind-up phonograph, and an old Philco radio.

The first set gets into gear around 7:30. The leader will give the downbeat in English—"oneandtwoandthreeandfour"—and off they go. The drummer will have a close-shaven head and he'll be wearing a baseball cap backward and basketball sneakers. The bassist will have a well-trimmed beard and be wearing a rumpled Italian suit and a Hawaiian shirt and he will be scrutinizing the world through steel-rimmed glasses. The piano player, wearing a gray sweatshirt, will be exceedingly loose. The leader, on the electric guitar, will be all in black and will announce each piece as either a "standard number" or "my original." His body action and grimaces as he soars with the music will be highly theatrical as he experiences a certain amount of difficulty with his amplifier, which is homemade. When they finish the set, the group will adjourn to a table in the corner.

A little kitchen (chef in bandana and wisp of a beard) turns out provender designed to quiet a hungry crowd. You might like to try the *shimeji no garlic oil spaghetti* (garlicky spaghetti with mushrooms) for ¥800, perhaps backed up by a tomato salad for ¥700 and a half bottle of Bordeaux for ¥2,000. The preferred drink here is bourbon, because bourbon is a hard-boiled, American, Jazz-in-a-boîte sort of tipple.

Two Jazz Coffeehouses

*The Tokyo jazz scene is also nurtured by little coffeehouses you can
drop in on to listen to non-stop recorded jazz from the owner's lovingly*

assembled collection. For the price of a cup of coffee, you can linger as long as you like. Two of the best are:

New Dug, near Shinjuku Station (tel: 3341-9339). First there was Dig, then there was Dug, then along came New Dug, sporting brick walls and bric-a-brac like the owner's dusty collection of antique time pieces and carriage clocks. The passing crowd settles in on the first and second floors while the habitués drift up to the quieter and more comfortable third. "French" coffee, ¥500. An "American" waffle, ¥400. Pizza, ¥800. New Dug, open until 2 a.m., is a remnant of the old Shinjuku, the preposterously alive neighborhood of 30 years ago. Now Mr. Tange's Town Hall has gone up and made us all respectable.

Mary Jane, near Shibuya Station (tel: 3461-3381). In a room as large as one side of a tennis court, there's this existential cafe, but without the existentialism. Windows shuttered like a country cottage, earnest original oils on the walls, and an arrangement of flowers of the field in the center of the large communal table. There are copies of Esquire and Playboy in Japanese and a rack of the Village Voice, which are more for atmosphere than for reading. Espresso, ¥500. A bacon and cheese sandwich, ¥700. A bowl of oatmeal, ¥600. Sometimes there's cheesecake from New York. Mary Jane is open until 11:30.

29 Shiatsu: More Than Massage

Oriental medicine holds that energy flows through the body but can get blocked if the body is not properly aligned. Acupuncture (in which very thin silver needles are inserted into the body at key junctions) and the burning of pinches of moxa (a substance obtained from the leaves of the wormwood plant) on the surface of the skin are two ways to attack the problem of blocked junctions. Shiatsu, in which the body is manipulated, is another.

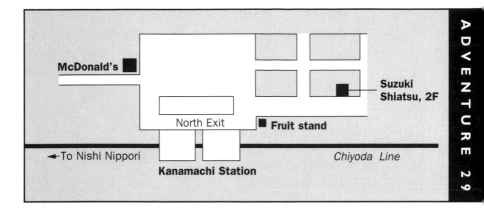

The techniques of shiatsu were developed in China well over a thousand years ago. The major school of shiatsu in Japan involves the practitioner's driving a knuckle or elbow into the patient's problem area and *wrenching* the body back into alignment. It can be painful, but for the most part, Japanese patients are inured. (Is it possible that a degree of masochism flavors the Japanese national character?)

Then 40 years ago along came Matsunaga-sensei with a revolutionary idea: shiatsu doesn't have to be painful. Matsunaga-sensei proceeded to found a new school of shiatsu, called "zen shiatsu," in which the body is *gently* manipulated. Matsunaga-sensei wrote an influential book about his school of shiatsu, which has been translated into English (*Zen Shiatsu*, Japan Publications).

As it happens, it is possible to put yourself into the hands of Matsunaga-sensei's direct descendent, Takeo Suzuki, the man Matsunaga chose to carry on his school after him. An hour-long session with Suzuki-sensei costs ¥6,000 (¥5,000 after the initial session) and is an extraordinary experience. After my first session I barely made it back to my home; I went straight to bed and slept for 16 hours. I have never been so relaxed in my life. Some people find the experience so enervating, they can't do anything meaningful for two or three days.

Call 3600-4204 to make an appointment for an hour's session. Clinic hours are 9 a.m. to 6 p.m., Tuesday through Saturday. The clinic is in Kanamachi, an unremarkable suburb out on the end of the

Chiyoda Line. Take the Yamanote Line to Nishi Nippori, where you change to the Chiyoda Line. Kanamachi is seven stops from Nishi Nippori.

The clinic is on the second floor of a building which also houses a *juku*, a cram school for kids preparing for their university entrance examinations. Take off your shoes in the *genkan* and in the little waiting room strip down to your underwear, stowing your clothes in a basket. Long-time patients wear flamboyantly colored track suits for a session, which they keep in a storage locker.

The clinic is essentially one room with a pale blue stamped-tin ceiling set with fluorescent lights. A green plant sulks in the corner and there is a delicate arrangement of flowers in the restroom. Suzuki-sensei's own charts of the meridian lines of energy flow in the body are posted on the wall—they look like monstrously complicated subway maps.

Heated mats are laid out for patients to wait on, covered with blankets. The first session involves Suzuki-sensei's getting to know your body. He seems to be disassembling you, picking up a part of your body, dusting it off, examining it from several angles, scribbling a note on his clipboard, then clicking the part back into place. He appears to be a mechanic faced with a malfunctioning piece of machinery which needs retuning. Or perhaps he is someone faced with the task of repacking a sloppily packed trunk.

He feels your abdomen, then a spot on your calf, and you discover that there must be a relation between the two. After an hour it is obvious that Suzuki-sensei knows far more about your body than you do—where it is tense, where it is discombobulated, where it lacks lubrication. He does not massage you so much as explore you, kneading and probing. He stretches you out, listening, feeling. After a while, you buckle, giving him complete control. Your neck is no longer capable of supporting your head, your backbone has no substance, your knees and legs seem to have only an incidental connection.

After your session, you are welcome to remain curled up in a semi-comatose state for as long as you like, until you can summon up sufficient resolve to climb back into your clothes and bid Suzuki-sensei a polite farewell.

On subsequent sessions, Suzuki-sensei will continue to explore your body in order to align it. Shiatsu affects people differently. Some people come once a week, some once a month. It may require many sessions to cure migraines, for instance. But even a single introductory session is illuminating.

Skiing Inside 30

You can do things in Tokyo that you can do in no other city. You can go trout fishing in Iidabashi. You can harvest rice in the Ginza. You can go parachuting in Suidobashi. In Tsurumi, you can go surfing on waves generated by a giant wave-making machine. In Nishi Funabashi, you can go skiing inside a huge purpose-built building, which is what this Little Adventure is all about.

Board the Keiyo Line local at its terminus, Tokyo Station, travel about 30 minutes, and get out at Minami Funabashi. You'll see from the station the gigantic structure where you are headed. It's half a kilometer long and looks like a moon rocket gantry tipped over on its side. It took four times as much steel to build as went into Tokyo Tower.

Most people when they first hear of this place, which calls itself **SSAWS Ski Dome** (SSAWS is Tokyo-speak for "Spring Summer Autumn Winter Snow"), they think it must be a mindless lark. But no, this is a serious effort by a major real estate company to use modern construction methods, computerized crowd-control techniques, and wizard snow-making technology to give skiers living in Tokyo a place they can well and truly ski, even at the height of a blistering Tokyo summer. Given that it's a considerable hassle to get from the city to the natural slopes in the northern prefectures, and that a weekend on those slopes can easily cost as much as a round-trip ticket to Los Angeles, it's no wonder that Ski Dome is a hit; it's not unusual to have 500 or more people on the slope or waiting to get on one of the two chair lifts.

Ski Dome's schedule is wonderfully arcane, and I set it down here to keep you from going all the way out to Nishi Funabashi, which in Tokyo terms is Nowheresville, for nothing. Ski Dome is closed for three days in April, June, September, and January for maintenance. Call 0474-32-7000 to check which days. Otherwise, on Monday, Tuesday, Wednesday, and Friday, it's snowboard-time exclusively from 8:30 to noon, after which it is exclusively ski-time until closing time at 10 p.m. On Thursday, it's skis from 10 a.m. to 6 p.m. and snowboards from 6 p.m. to 10 p.m. On the weekends and national holidays, it's snowboards from 8 until noon and skis from noon until 10 p.m. God knows what the schedule would look like if a third way to slither down a bank of snow were to become popular.

The pricing is almost as complicated. A full-day pass costs ¥5,400 for adults, which means a morning of snowboarding and an after-noon and evening of skiing, or vice versa. There are a number of hearties who actually do this (and there is no hearty like a Japanese hearty—they wear their ski-goggles down while grabbing a quick beer at the slope-side cafe), and by six o'clock many of them can be seen slumped over on a bench in a corridor in full ski regalia, too whipped even to take their boots off. The more usual routine is to sign up for the "Time Pass System," which involves paying a ¥2,200 admission fee, then ¥250 for every 15 minutes spent on the slope during the hours of your preferred sport, which you pay for when you leave Ski Dome because your magnetized admission ticket will have been tracked by the computer every time you go through one of the numerous barriers.

On top of this, you will have to rent ski clothes and gear, if you don't bring your own. It is no good thinking you can get away with a pair of old jeans and an L.L. Bean sweater. It's cold on the slope, minus 3 or 4 degrees centrigrade, so you'll need proper equipment—anyway, you won't be allowed on the slope if you aren't properly turned out. Unthinkable.

It will cost you ¥1,800 to rent the whole shebang, which is embroidered with the Ski Dome logo and has been cleaned anew after the previous renter turned it in. Perhaps 10 percent of the skiers at Ski Dome rent clothes; most have their own up-to-date, razzle-dazzle ski clothes which they probably bought at one of the dozen or so ski shops inside Ski Dome.

Ski rental will cost you another ¥1,800 (there are 1,300 pairs to choose from), boots ¥1,200, and poles ¥500. You only need buy ski-boot socks if you haven't brought your own, but you can buy a pair with the Ski Dome logo for ¥1,200 at the Pro Shop. The shop will also polish your edges and wax your bottoms for ¥2,000; rental skis won't need this as they are kept sparkling by the maintenance staff.

The cost to rent snowboards and associated gear is similar.

So at last, properly decked out, you're ready to make your entrance on the slope. Follow the signs to "Gelände," which is what Ski Dome calls the slope. Line up for the four-person chair lift going up the left of the slope if you are a hotshot, or for the chair lift on the right if you'd prefer to feel your way into this thing. The 100-meter-wide slope is clearly partitioned off to let the experienced skiers do their stuff without having to watch out for klutzes. The Ski Patrol is there to keep the crazies in line but in general there is a strong sense of discipline for the sake of public order.

In one corner, the Ski School, color photographs of whose handsome instructors are posted in the lobby, demonstrates the snow plow. Pop music burbles in the background. The snow is remarkably fine, a new layer being put down every night after the slope closes.

When you feel like a break, pass through the turnstile and the computer will recognize that you are no longer to be charged slope time. An air compressor is available so you can blow ice off your bindings, and tools are available for a quick tuneup. Adjourn to one of the several restaurants and cafes and get yourself around a pizza, a curry, or a bowl of noodles. (You'll never be too far from the slope; there are 90 TV sets throughout Ski Dome showing who's coming down at any moment.)

Some rent a video camera to take back out on the slope. Bored souls take to the video game room and some others just give up and adjourn to a sauna, then go for a swim in the heated pool (rental of swimsuit with Ski Dome logo: ¥500).

After a few visits to Ski Dome (season tickets are available), you come to think it perfectly natural to spend a summer afternoon in what appears to be the long lobby of an international airport, with everyone clumping by in the stiff-kneed Frankenstein gait of people clamped into ski boots. Hint: to avoid the peak crowds, go on a week-day, preferably in *winter*.

3 | Miniature Formula-1 Car Racing

In Tokyo, the Walter Mitty dream of driving a high-speed racing car is catered to by video games in which you view the course through three-dimensional glasses and you feel a jitter if the wheels go off the road. In the United States, you can come close to the real thing with a Malibu Grand Prix racer, a scaled-up version of a go-cart. In Ebina, about 40 minutes from Yokohama on an express train of the Sotetsu Line, you can come even closer.

At **Formula Club** in Ebina, you can screech around a tight racing course in a two-thirds scale Formula-1 racing car built by Suzuki Engineering, the people who build the real thing. The cars, powered by two-stroke aluminum snowmobile engines made by Yamaha, are theoretically able to hit 160 kph, but they are fitted here with a gover-nor which limits them to 120 kph. However, the demands of this tricky little track (the longest straight, the back stretch, is only about 150 meters long) mean that you can't crank it up to much over 30 kph without spinning out on a tight turn. Still, 30 kph around this course in one of these precision machines, pushing it to the limit and taking the optimum line through the corners, feels as though you're hitting 240 kph. You may find the experience addictive.

The last time we visited Formula Club, the Porsche Owners' Club of Japan had rented the facilities for the morning. We watched them put the cars through their paces and it was obvious that the drivers were being challenged. The most skillful of the Porsche drivers were pulling down lap times of 55 seconds, while the young lady at the club's reception desk told us she could do it in 50. (The course record is 48.070 seconds at time of writing. Lap times, and even section times within the lap, are recorded digitally to three places and printed out for all drivers for subsequent painstaking analysis.)

As we sat in lawn chairs on the club's grassy veranda which overlooks the course, we sipped soft drinks and studied the techniques of the Porsche owners. The steering of these cars is one revolution lock to lock, and the smallest movement of the steering wheel is directly translated to the front wheels. The brakes are hair-trigger and the acceleration, once the fluid transmission takes hold, will throw you hard back against the bucket seat. You are strapped in across the waist and have nylon belts across each shoulder. You must wear a fireproof face mask and a racing helmet, both of which can be provided. Some drivers don racing coveralls, shoes, and gloves.

The cost of one "round" is ¥4,000 for non-members, one round consisting of five separately timed circuits of the track, each from a standing start. Drivers are not allowed to pass another car or even come close to another car on the circuit. As the cars have no gears, the skill comes only in being able to find the groove and use the brakes not to slow the car, but to set the car in the best position to attack the upcoming curve.

The course is carefully monitored and nobody has ever been injured; the worst that can happen is that you will spin out, in which case the pit crew will have to push your car back on the course, as the cars do not have reverse gears. (If you spin out twice, you will have to leave the course: the thing is, if you are going to haul down a reasonably competitive lap time, you must develop a sense of how hard you can push the car—what the limits are—and to do this you must push the car over the limit.)

You will quickly learn that these cars, even though gearless, are no toys. Real skill is involved here. It is said that you must drive at least 100 rounds before you will be able to approach a 50-second lap time, and that you must keep your skills honed by regular practice. Every evening the course is open under lights, and this is when the experienced drivers come out to practice.

Formula Club has 550 paid members and there are now five different circuits open to them, with Ebina being the closest to Tokyo. The idea is that motor sports should not be limited to spectators, that the real thrill is in participation.

The club needs to see your driver's license before they can let you on the track, so be sure to bring it. Telephone 0462-38-5212.

32 Sumida River Dinner Cruise

There is nothing quite so Old Edo as an evening cruise in a *yakata-bune*, a Sumida River houseboat, with an elegant but casual *bento*, some good saké, and a few good friends. Depending on when you go, you can drift by thousands of cherry trees in bloom on the banks, or you can watch the spectacular mid-summer fireworks just as in the old woodblock prints, or at *Obon* you can inscribe a paper lantern to the memory of one who has gone before and float it with hundreds of others on the river, watching until it disappears in the night, or you can just go out to view the moon—*tsukimi*. No excuse is needed, really.

The best of the river boats are run by **Komatsuya**, who entered the business in Showa 2 (1927). Komatsuya's boats are about 40 feet long and are finely crafted of Japanese cypress, with copper fittings and tatami throughout. As you sit on the tatami you are just a couple of feet off the water.

To celebrate other times, some of your fellow passengers may dress in *yukata* and *geta*. There is congenial confusion when it's time to board, particularly if other boats are leaving at the same time, but eventually everybody finds a place along the low banquet table which runs the length of the boat. Only a little late, the boat slips under the bridge out of the Kanda River and into the Sumida. The red lanterns hanging from the eaves swing gently—we are a floating *akachochin*. *Bento* boxes are passed down the table and the beer and saké are broken out. A river breeze causes the shoji to flutter.

A jolly lady in kimono installed at the head of the table switches on a microphone, introduces herself, and begins to tell of passing bridges, famous buildings, and ancient trysts. She is only momentarily silenced by a terrific rumble from the Sobu Line as it clatters over us, packed with commuters.

A *suijo* (bus ferry) strides purposefully by up the river. Huge rooftop signs begin to flicker: Hitachi, Fuji Film, Tokyo Gas. Lots of construction. Tokyo is not yet finished. No, not yet begun. How sad that the city is cut off from this magnificent river. Edo was not like this. Back then there were restaurants and teahouses right down to the water.

The bridges are wonderful constructions, each embodying a different architectural approach, each painted a different color. The wind out here is soft and sweet, not of the city.

We sidle down past Tsukudajima and leave the river to ease out into the great harbor. Past Nakanoshima. Spotting us as a pleasure boat, a seagull tags along.

We see the lights of Korakuen baseball stadium and hear the distant mumble of the crowd. Past the IHI shipyards, black tankers high out of the water, like beached hippos. Past the navy yard, dark and not large. We are now out in the working harbor, ships at anchor all around us.

Look—Fuji! We can see Mt. Fuji! Spontaneous applause for this great piece of theater.

Tokyo Tower lights up. Off the starboard quarter is downtown Tokyo. Alongside Takeshiba Pier lie the boats for the islands. They will leave later this evening, around ten. As the sun goes down, Toshiba headquarters seems a paper cutout against the glowing sky. Past an island where nobody lives. Another *yakatabune* joins us and we skip along together. She shows us how festive we must look, our lanterns bobbing. We hear their laughter over the water. Past Suijo-koen, where young couples come at night to lie together in the grass. A clutch of dogged wind surfers.

Karaoke time, hoho. This is no quiet, contemplative evening: this is rowdy old Tokyo, out here on the water.

Now it is dark. We've been out for over an hour. We seem to be floating on a great darkness, detached from the earth. We begin to sing and clap slowly to the rhythm, which matches the gentle rock of the boat. We cruise for a bit, then, in a wide arc, turn back. Back past the huge signs, back up the Sumidagawa, into the Kanda.

Komatsuya's address is Higashi Nihonbashi 2-27-22 (tel: 3851-2780), and the nearest train stop is Bakuro-cho on the Sobu Line.

You'll need to put together a party of at least ten people. The cost will be ¥15,000 each, which includes a tempura dinner. You can buy beer and saké on the boat or you can bring your own. The classic time to take the trip is when the cherry trees are in bloom, but all boats are in heavy demand at this time, of course.

PART FIVE *Listen, I Found This Great Place…*

In spite of the liveliness of its streets and the openness of its old neighborhoods, Tokyo is no more a public city than, say, Paris or New York. Many of the most congenial places are tiny and hidden away down anonymous alleys, with no identifying signs. Because in many cases you have to be introduced, these little places are like private clubs and it can take some time for a newcomer to the city to sort it all out.

Well, just come with me.

Iidabashi on the Chuo Line is one of the few areas of Tokyo that more or less survived the fire bombs of the Great Pacific War. (Uguisudani, "Nightingale Valley," is another.) It is pleasant to wander the twisting cobblestone alleys of Iidabashi and imagine how it must have been.

There is a high incidence of *ryotei* in the neighborhood. *Ryotei* are elegant establishments of great circumspection at which geisha serve intricate meals to company presidents and others with influence and generous expense accounts. A meal at an Iidabashi *ryotei* can easily cost ¥50,000 but you can spend an hour or two at **Iseto**, a wonderful *nomiya* (literally, "drink shop") right in the middle of the area, for not a lot more than ¥2,000.

A visit to a *nomiya* like Iseto is the classic way to begin a Tokyo evening—*nomiya* are what displaced Tokyoites are missing when they say they are homesick—but one doesn't go to a *nomiya* to eat so much as to muse with friends about the curious ways of the world, all the while sipping premium saké and sampling a series of small snacks designed to complement the saké. Dinner is afterward.

Iseto (tel: 3260-6363) is located at Kagurazaka 4-2, Shinjuku-ku. Hours are from 5 p.m. to 9:30 p.m.—it's best to arrive early. Push aside the short rope curtain and creak open the frail wooden door. You will be met with a muted chorus of *"Irasshaimase,"* a more modulated welcome than the greeting bellowed out at most *nomiya*. Iseto is not rowdy. The interior is so softly lit that shadows are cast. There is a secluded rock garden, two six-mat tatami rooms with small tables and cushions, and a low counter seating six. Sit at the counter if you are in the mood to be in the middle of things; sit in one of the tatami rooms (*ozashiki*) if you are with friends and in a more reclusive mood.

Either way, as soon as you are seated your waitress, who is dressed in the casual home wear of a hundred years ago, will bring you an *oshibori* towel for you to refresh your face and wipe the dust from your hands, and this will automatically be followed by the *otoshi*, a set course of five dishes which change daily. The *otoshi* costs ¥1,500 and might include, for example, *shiokara*, salted strips of squid in a sauce distilled from squid innards; *rakkyo*, pickled Japanese onions; a dish of inch-long shrimp mixed with *shirasuboshi*, an even tinier fish; or slices of the giant Japanese radish called *daikon* simmered in soy sauce, saké, rice vinegar, and a pinch of sugar. Almost always included is a lacquer bowl of *miso shiru*, the pungent soy-based soup with mushrooms and tofu which is the centerpiece of a traditional Japanese breakfast.

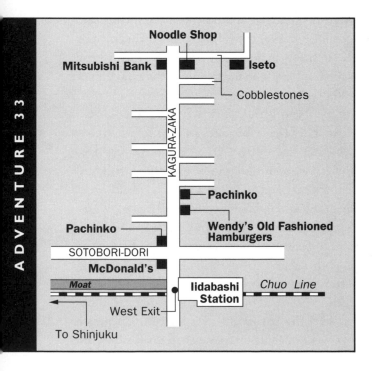

Your waitress will inquire: *"Onominomo wa?"* ("And to drink?")
The choice is simple: there is only Japanese saké and of that only one
kind, Haku Taka ("White Hawk"), a noble potion made in Nada, the
most famous saké-brewing area in Japan. Haku Taka is dry with a lingering aftertaste and is dispensed from the great straw-covered container perched on the edge of the counter.

So your only decision is whether to have your saké heated, *kan*, or
at room temperature, *hiya*. This is a matter of preference and mood,
but think: would you subject a fine wine to heat, even if, as at Iseto, it
is lovingly and most carefully coddled in water warmed over charcoal
to skin temperature and no higher? However you order your saké, a
flagon costs ¥500, not at all expensive. Succeeding rounds will be
accompanied by a little dish of something additional to nibble on.

On your little table you will find a paper-thin sliver of wood on
which ten additional snacks have been written with a brush. This
menu changes little except when the seasons change, and will probably include dishes like *natto* (fermented soybean with slices of scallion
and the yolk of quail's egg), *maruboshi* (a trio of fat sardines), *tatami
iwashi* (tiny sardines dried and pressed flat to look vaguely like a tatami mat), and *inago* (crunchy grasshoppers which have been simmered
for days in *tsukudani*, a sort of Japanese chutney). These dishes cost
around ¥300 each and are tried and true *nomiya* staples, but you need
not feel obliged to order any of them if you are not in the mood.

Iseto's master, Kameyama Kame, keeps a magisterial grip on the
proceedings. He will admonish you to lower your voice if he feels you
are talking too loudly. As a result, conversations take on a conspirato-
rial air and a comforting intimacy descends. On the hour, the old
clock on the wall chimes; from time to time a customer will gently
jangle the bell which is placed on every table to relieve one of the
need to call for a waitress, and soon it seems utterly natural to communicate in murmurs, the pauses growing longer and longer as time
gradually loosens its grip.

Iseto is closed Sundays and holidays, and you should know that
they've never heard of credit cards.

34 Radio Bar

Tokyo's oldest bar, Kamiya Bar in Asakusa, opened its doors in 1889 and soon gained a reputation for its home-brewed concoction called Denki Bran, "Electric Brandy." In the years since, Tokyo has evolved a distinctive bar culture. Tokyo bars are by and large highly polished places, conscious of their roots in a Western institution, staffed by serious students of the history and literature of the cocktail who take pride in being able to offer a selection of well-tuned potables, a portion of which will be intriguingly esoteric. A top-level Tokyo bar is not so much a place to drink alcohol to jack up the spirit as to engage in an almost religious ritual which sets off those participating as sophisticates versed in the ways of the world.

A visit to **Radio Bar**, which may be the most polished bar of them all, is an experience to be relished. I once took a jaded friend from New York to Radio Bar and it was the only place in Tokyo that he found impressive. He even bought a copy of Radio Bar's own book for ¥3,600, which has beautiful photographs of Radio Bar's cocktails in glasses borrowed from collectors and museums.

Radio Bar opens at 7 p.m. (except on Sundays and holidays), but it is very quiet until people begin drifting in after dinner. Come a little before 9 p.m. to be assured of one of the nine leather-covered bar stools at the long cherry-wood counter. There are three, sometimes four bartenders in attendance, in wing collars and black vests, which must be the highest bartender/drinker ratio of any bar in the world.

A brass plate holding a thick *oshibori* towelette/napkin will be set before you. Leaf through the leather-bound list of suggestions. There are old standards like the Daiquiri, the Stinger, the Negroni, the Mint Julep, and the Brandy Alexander; there are Radio Bar creations like the Greta Garbo (gin, dry vermouth, and dry sherry) and the Diane Keaton (white wine, gin, and Pernod); and there are drinks made with *eaux de vie* and the juice of a fruit in season—peach or water-

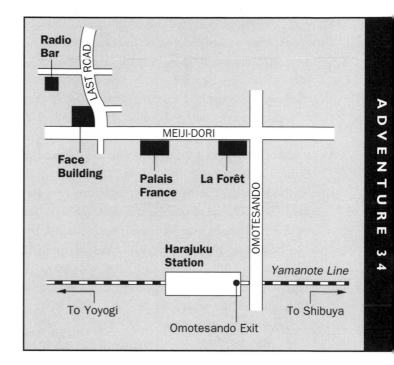

melon in summer, grape in the fall. There is a dazzling selection of 60 or so fine malt whiskeys, like 1940 Glenlivet (at ¥10,000 the measure), and a line of ancient ports.

The cocktails, although they go for a stiff ¥1,500, are small, as if to emphasize their exquisiteness. Radio Bar is no place for two-fisted drinkers. The advantage of this is that nobody gets excited, the conversation is always listenable. If you are thirsty you might consider ordering a split (¥7,000) or a bottle (¥13,000) of Veuve Cliquot yellow label. It will be poured into a chilled Rosenthal or Baccarat flute glass engraved with the house insignia.

You will be served a platter of non-obvious things to nibble on for the ¥1,500 cover charge: things like apricots, dried grapes (not the same as raisins), roast pistachios, maybe a slice of an unusual cheese. It is possible also to order a light meal like an omelette (¥1,000 to ¥1,200) and a green salad (¥1,000).

Radio Bar was designed *twice* by Isamu Wakabayashi, a noted sculptor. After he designed it the first time, he took to drinking there. As he drank he thought how he could make the space more striking. Finally he asked Radio Bar's owner, Koji Ozaki, if he could redo it and Ozaki said, "Why not?" The result is magnificent: crinkled steel walls, that thick cherry counter with a brass foot railing, an array of pinpoint lights set into the ceiling, an art deco lamp at the end of the counter, a panoply of back-lit bottles and an antique carriage clock behind the bar, and a brilliant outburst of flowers in a soft spotlight. In a space inset into the wall, a perfectly preserved radio from the twenties.

From 9 to 12, the atmosphere is that of a well-mannered cocktail party. Those without a seat at the bar simply stand. By midnight, people are beginning to drift away. Only those with little to do the next day remain until the 2 a.m. closing time. When you pay your bill, your change will be returned in crisp new notes on a silver salver. Radio Bar, you should be warned, recognizes no plastic, which seems, somehow, absolutely in character.

Radio Bar (tel: 3405-5490) is located at Jingumae 2-31-7.

35   Banana Split, Tokyo Style

An old-fashioned Tokyo dessert, concocted on the premises of a shop which has remained unchanged since the thirties, is the gentlest divertissement imaginable. The shop I have in mind is called **Takemura** and it is just two blocks away from that assault on the senses called Akihabara. Also in the neighborhood are four of Tokyo's most characterful traditional restaurants and the Transportation Museum, which has what must be the world's largest train layout.

Take the Marunouchi line to Awajicho and leave by Exit A3. You will recognize Takemura and Isegen, the wonderful anglerfish-stew restaurant across the street from Takemura, because both buildings are perfectly preserved wooden structures from early Showa. Imagine what an endearing city Tokyo must have been when all its buildings were of this style.

Duck through Takemura's crisp linen *noren* and slide open the door. The waitresses will murmur, *"Irrashaimase,"* and Mr. Hotta, the present proprietor and son of the founder, will rasp out the same from the back of the shop where he will be tending a vintage machine which pounds rice into a cool granite cauldron to make *mochi.*

Wax models of the choices available are on display in a glass case to make it easier for you to make up your mind, but I can't imagine your not taking a liking to the Kuriimu-Anmitsu—honey bean paste with ice cream and sufficient garnishes to light up a Christmas tree—for ¥600.

Take a seat at one of the little tables or pull up a cushion on the tatami area, whichever suits your mood.

A waitress in jeans and an immaculate smock embroidered with the house insignia will bring you a cup of *sakurayu*, salted water with a lightly pickled cherry blossom floating in it. The saltiness sets you up for the sweetness which will follow, just as in the tea ceremony a sweetcake sets you up for the bitter tea that comes later.

A wooden tray with a bowl of Kuriimu-Anmitsu, a miniature jug of molasses syrup, and a cup of green tea is placed before you. Pour the syrup over everything, thereby participating in a small way in the preparation. The bowl of Kuriimu-Anmitsu contains a small scoop of homemade vanilla ice cream, a scoop of honeyed bean paste, a scattering of cubes of clear jelly, a few slices of *mikan* orange, some sugared fruit jellybabies, a sprinkling of sweet beans for texture, and a stemmed cherry—a celebration of innocent sweetness. When you have finished, as the dessert leaves a cloying aftertaste, sip the green tea to cut the lingering sweetness.

Takemura is no faded relic of the past: it does a brisk business, at least partly because being here is so relaxing. There are no printed posters, no music, no harsh lights, no insistent colors. People tend to linger, talking softly. On festival days such as the New Year holidays and on Seijin-no-hi, when a new crop of Tokyoites turns 20 years old, Takemura will be filled with young ladies in brilliant kimono, because there is no pastime quite so Old Tokyo as a short break for something sweet at the shop called Takemura.

Takemura is closed Sundays and holidays, but is otherwise open until 8 p.m.

36 Drunkard's Alley

Cozy little drinking places with seats for only five or six reasonably svelte customers, looked after by an expansive character who is a bit of a renegade, are an old Tokyo tradition. It's to places like this that a large portion of the (male) population repairs at the end of the day to wash down a few skewers of *yakitori* with a flask or two of saké, while discussing strategies and building alliances. As the clientele settle in over the years, these places tend to develop their own niches, so that one will find itself home to political journalists and cartoonists, another will tend to attract people interested in building and flying experimental aircraft, and another will cater to mountaineers. In this way, they are like little clubs.

Unfortunately, very unfortunately, these little places are now under terrific pressure, as the economics of running an establishment with just six seats in a city whose real estate is worth as much as all of the real estate in the U.S. makes no sense at all. We've already lost "The Street of Dreams" in Shinbashi to developers and Shinjuku's wonderful Golden Gai is almost gone. Luckily, **Nonbei Yokocho** ("Drunkards' Alley") just across the street from Shibuya Station seems safe for the moment as the 39 little places that make it up are jammed together on a very narrow strip of land bounded on one side by the Yamanote Line

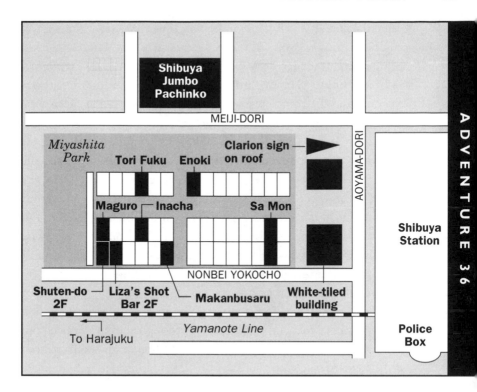

and on the other by the cemented-over Kanda River, an awkwardness which has so far deflected the interest of the developers.

An evening in one of the little places in Nonbei Yokocho is bound to be memorable. You should be aware that not all of these places are eager to welcome foreign faces, especially early in the evening, because they feel that foreigners speaking their peculiar languages will be difficult to communicate with and may put other customers off. As a matter of protocol, therefore, it is probably not a good idea to come with a fellow foreigner and spend the whole evening talking to each other. It's cooler as well as more of an adventure if you go alone on your first visit and do more listening than talking. Then the next time you drop in you'll be welcomed as a member in good standing. Here are five places in Nonbei Yokocho which you will find particularly congenial and at which you will be welcome right from the start, if only as a curiosity. None of them is expensive; you'll find it hard to spend much more than ¥3,000.

1. **Tori Fuku** ("Happy Bird"). The taciturn Mr. Murayama roasts over charcoal the complete *yakitori* repertoire, including *tamago no michi* (bird's unlaid eggs), *sunagimo* (gizzard), and *tebasaki* (wings). His superb *sasami* (breast) comes wrapped around a *shiso* leaf and is eaten dipped into grated *daikon* thickened with a quail's egg, and the meal is finished off with a cup of herbal homemade potato soup, the perfect grace note. Ms. Murayama (sister) presides over the annex upstairs, which is reached by a staircase an narrow as a ladder. Tori Fuku was established 40 years ago by Mr. Murayama's father, who started the business using a *yatai*, a street cart. Such is the rapport built up by the senior Murayama: his old customers still drop by, often to introduce their grandsons.

2. **Liza's Shot Bar**. Liza's about 28 years old and is thus the new wave of Nonbei Yokocho proprietors. Although she's never been out of the country, she speaks perfect English. Reggae and soul spill out of the cassette player on the bar. She serves moussaka, taramo salad, and French bread for ¥1,000, and when she's in the mood she'll whip up a batch of frozen Margaritas. Decorations are in a whatever-will-be-will-be mode, with graffiti and tiger skins and an almost critical mass of clutter. The house phone is cordless.

3. **Enoki**. Chizuru-san, Enoki's pert and lively proprietor, is so open and jolly you will feel at home immediately. She holds her ground against the banter with the assurance of a stand-up comedian. In tribute, all her patrons, from the justice of the Supreme Court on down, call her "Mama." This is a high-class place. The keep bottles are malt whiskey, the plates are chosen with care, and Chizuru is an imaginative cook on her single gas burner behind the counter.

4. **Inacha** has been presided over for the past 40 years by Ms. Matsumoto. She wears a crisp kimono and drinks whiskey while you drink saké so that as the evening unwinds it's a race to see who can

get loosest fastest. In a very simple setting, Ms. Matsumoto serves things like boiled new baby potatoes or *matsutake* mushroom rice in season, with her own pickles in support. Ms. Matsumoto likes to watch television, so the conversation is mostly counterpoint to what's on the screen. Identify Nacha by its rope *noren* out front.

5. **Makanbusaru.** Setsuko (68) has been running this place for 26 years. Its name commemorates the town in Indonesia where her sister lived during the war. There's a map of Indonesia on the wall and a mobile of Japanese fighter planes. This is a place for people with a history behind them to come and reminisce over saké and *shochu*. Setsuko's offerings are simple: tofu, spinach, *natto*. Toward the end of the evening an ex-corporal of the now defunct Imperial Army, a sweet old guy, might drop in to play a few requests for the songs he specializes in, songs dripping with nostalgia, on his guitar. Other places shoo him away but he's at home here.

6. **Shuten-do.** Enter through the aluminum door and make your way up an almost vertical staircase not quite as wide as your shoulders. The dim-lit room, as large as a walk-in closet, recalls a submarine. As you sit at the bar, the window behind you looks out on a little park and the other off to your right has a fine view of passing Yamanote Line trains. There is a range of classic malt whiskeys from ¥900 to ¥1,200 and there's homemade pizza, which gets delivered all over the neighborhood. People with an interest in the theater tend to congregate here. It's almost always open until 5 in the morning, so this is a good place to wait for the trains to start running again.

7. **Yasaiya.** One of the newer places in Nonbei Yokocho, run by two vivacious young women who have traveled the world and now want to introduce what they have discovered to their contemporaries. The food is Mediterranean—ratatouille, salad Niçoise, garlic bread—and the talk lively. Up the stairs in Yasaiya is a small tatami room perfect for an (intimate) party, a branch of Shuten-do.

8. **Sa Mon.** One of the most popular places in Nonbei Yokocho, partly because of its outgoing Mama-san. It's also the largest, seating maybe 15. The atmosphere is something like a miniature German

beer hall—busy, noisy, with flashes of ribaldry. Try to get there early, as the place fills up as soon as the offices let out. People usually don't begin to leave until well into the evening.

9. **Maguro**. You'll be asked to take off your shoes and leave them outside, but this is as fastidious as Maguro gets. The place is less evocative of Tokyo than the Deep South, with an intensity level of zero on a scale of ten. The house specialty is sashimi, but if you would like a platter of oden, somebody will go next door to get it for you at the place Maguro supplies its sashimi to on call, a common arrangement in Nonbei Yokocho. The second floor is a three-mat tatami room where not so long ago eight people congregated for a party that is still being talked about.

10. **The Clarion Sign**. As you make your way back to Shibuya Station, you might pause for a few seconds to take in the sign up on the top of a building by Clarion, a manufacturer of car audio systems. Clarion apparently sunk its entire advertising budget into this one sign, which is composed of miles of shimmering neon, making this the most complex neon sign in the world.

37 A Perfect Cup of Coffee

It is said that at the turn of the century the government of Brazil began shipping a steady supply of top-grade coffee beans to Japan—gratis. Whoever decided to do this was a marketing genius. Now, although Japan began drinking coffee a good hundred years later than Europe and the Americas, the Japanese consume more coffee than any nation except the United States, Germany, and France, and most of it is the pick of the crop. The Japanese have never learned how to drink the rough stuff.

In Tokyo, coffeehouses abound—over 15,000 at last count—and

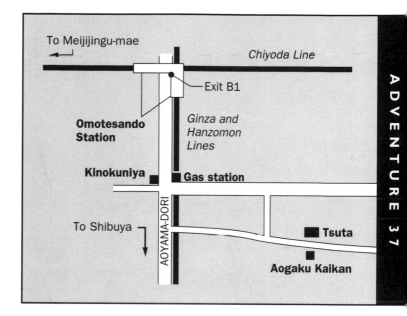

they constitute a real Tokyo institution. In the days when few people had hi-fi equipment in their homes, you could listen to whole Wagnerian operas at a coffeehouse for the price of a single cup. Some people even brought scores. The present-day Tokyo coffeehouses have more in common with the coffeehouses of Vienna and 18th century London: quiet shelter for as long as you like offering a place to read, talk, write letters, and wait for the world to turn your way.

These days many coffeehouses are quite splendid. The Cafe La Mille coffeehouse chain has 37 shops, all furnished with European antiques, where you are given a choice of Royal Copenhagen, Limoges, Ginoli, or Sevres chinaware. The decor of the Cafe Le Temps in the Ginza evokes Paris of the twenties, with chairs, tables, paintings and *objets d'art* from the private collection of the owner, a renowned connoisseur.

The carte of places like this tends to cover several pages, allowing you to choose among beans from all the world's great bean-growing regions. The most expensive cup is always Blue Mountain from Jamaica, which in upscale places will go for at least ¥1,000, often more.

But you can easily find these places yourself. Here I want to introduce you to a coffeehouse you probably wouldn't run across yourself in the ordinary way. **Tsuta** ("Ivy") is in a private house right next to Aoyama Gakuin University, just off Aoyama-Dori. At the ivy-covered entrance there is the wooden sign

蔦
珈
琲
店

which means "Tsuta Coffeehouse."

Inside there are two tables and a long counter. The tables are nice, as they look out on a garden as manicured as a putting green, which is softly illuminated in the evening, but you might also enjoy sitting at the counter and watching how your cup is brewed.

At Tsuta there is no variation for variation's sake. The house coffee bean is from Brazil—Santos No.2, Screen 18. You can order *café au lait* (¥600) or the intense demitasse (¥700) or iced coffee (¥600), but for your first cup, you might just ask for *kohi*, the basic ¥500 cup of coffee. An almost religious ritual will unfold. A saucer and gold-plated spoon will be placed before you, as well as a brass container of sugar and, from the refrigerator, one of cream.

The beans for your cup, artfully roasted on the premises twelve hours previously so they will have a chance to recover, are ground, not too finely. A pot of water which has been run through a filter is brought to a boil. (Bottled mineral water is used at Tsuta only to make tea. Taiji Koyama, Tsuta's proprietor, thinks mineral water is too bland for coffee.)

Thirty grams of ground beans are spooned into a fine linen filter pocket about the size of a fist, the linen having been woven to house specifications and the filter having been carefully rinsed after every cup. The boiling water is then poured into another pot with a spout like the neck of a swan, and some hot water is also poured into the cup that will contain your coffee, to warm it.

Boiling water is now very carefully dribbled over the beans in the filter. The dribbling process takes two or three minutes and requires the undivided attention of the master technician behind the counter. The effect is that your coffee is handcrafted.

The hot water is poured out of your cup and your cup is wiped dry with a linen cloth. Finally, the drip of Santos No.2, Screen 18, is reverently poured into your cup, and your cup is placed on the saucer before you.

The music at Tsuta is mostly Mozart, sometimes Bach, or Chopin. Mozart is best for coffee drinking, conversing, and gazing at the garden thinks Mr.Koyama.

Two More Coffeehouses

While Tsuta is quiet, private, and unassuming, Bon and Cafe George V, both in Shinjuku a couple of minutes from the station, are somewhat more spectacular coffeehouses which have still managed to retain the requisite coziness. If I had to make a TV documentary about Tokyo coffeehouses, Bon and George V would have to figure.

Bon has 450 different sets of cups and saucers on display behind its long counter, all of them of museum quality. There is a shelf of Meisen and another of Royal Copenhagen, and the rest are Japanese. You may choose, if you like.A cup of the house blend or Brazil or Moka or Columbia costs ¥950 while a cup of Blue Mountain is ¥1,300. Yes, it's expensive, but this means that Bon is never crowded.

Your cup is placed before you with the kind of soulful precision one sees at a tea ceremony. Set to the side is a polished copper bowl of granulated sugar, a silver creamer of "vegetable" cream, and a copper creamer with bovine cream. Bach or Chopin issues from oversized Quad speakers and at one end of the counter you are likely to spot one of Bon's dedicated acolytes sorting through a tray of beans, looking for imperfection.

To get to Bon, leave Shinjuku Station by the East Exit and turn left. Cross the street to the two-story-high TV screen labeled "Studio Alta." Turn left. Bon is 75 meters along this street, its entrance marked by a discreet wooden sign.

Cafe George V *is down a flight of wooden stairs with a very slight warp to them. Just inside the door is an illuminated display case with cups and saucers labeled Spode 1935, Wedgewood 1900, and Royal Worchester 1880. On the old tables are exuberant displays of flowers, leather volumes, and antique coffee-making equipment. There is a marble bust in the corner, frosted-glass panels, and oil paintings and etchings of European cities on the walls. A gentle lady in a long black skirt and a white silk blouse will take your order for a cup of blend,* café au lait, *or* cafe glacé *for ¥500. A slice of one of the cakes for which the place has a reputation is ¥600.*

To get to George V, take the East Exit of Shinjuku Station, turn right, and go to the end of the station building. Cross the street to Chuo-Dori street. George V is 30 meters down Chuo-Dori on the right. There's a small sign on the side of the "Hole in the Wall" spaghetti restaurant pointing the way.

38   Tempura Iseya

Iseya is a wonderful old-line tempura shop in one of the few parts of town to escape the ravages of the war. Most of the buildings are two-story and the pace is noticeably more relaxed than in areas of the town where buildings cast long shadows. The sliding front doors of houses here exit immediately onto the street, and on the stoops there are probably cats and almost certainly miniature forests of potted plants. There are open, comfortably cluttered shops on every block selling necessities to the neighborhood. There is a smattering of small

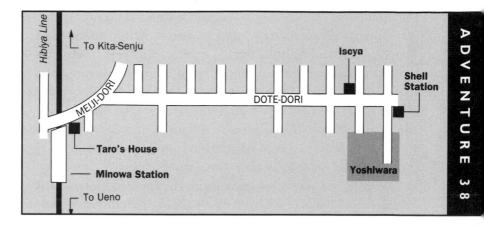

factories that pick up and deliver in battered mini-vans. There's a nice old public bath and an ancient, ivy-covered police box.

Everyone knows where Iseya is. It's the neighborhood tempura joint. People come on bicycles and the youngest of the family is wheeled in, in a stroller. Because Iseya takes no reservations, there's usually a line of half a dozen or so, but nobody minds waiting for a few minutes as everybody knows everybody else and it is an occasion for a little gossip. It also allows time to inspect Iseya's marvelous facade: a globe of light above the sliding door, an awning cranked up and down by a chain, and "TEMPURA ISEYA" above the door in gilded *kanji*, each of which is sheltered under its individual roof.

Inside, the floor is stone. There are four low wooden tables with benches and in the back, two small tables on tatami. There are light bulbs in old-fashioned fixtures (when one of the fixtures breaks, the master orders a replacement from a factory in Hokkaido that still makes them: his instinct is to preserve). There are a few period advertisements on the wall and an old clock. On the tables, the *shoyu* (soy sauce) containers are antiques.

Iseya's tempura is rough and ready, Edo style, heavy on the soy sauce. It is not served to you piece by piece as in the lofty tempura establishments in the Ginza, but all scrapped together in a savory mass, like a Mexican omelet. It is very filling.

An honest, blue-collar dish is *kaki-age donburi* (¥1,500)—tempura shrimp, scallops, and vegetables on a bowl of rice. More elegant in appearance, but essentially the same thing, is *tenju* (¥1,500), which comes in a lacquer box instead of a bowl. You can also order a platter of mixed tempura (again, pretty much the same thing) for ¥2,500 and for another ¥200 have a bowl of *gohan* (rice) on the side. Round out the meal with a ¥450 dish of hearty turnip and *daikon* pickles and afterward, perhaps, a bowl of *miso shiru* or, if you're feeling fancy, a ¥200 bowl of *namekojiru* with *nameko* mushrooms.

When Kyoto people complain about the *koi* (dark) taste of Tokyo food, Iseya's tempura is what they are talking about. Iseya's customers, on the other hand, would find Kyoto-style tempura, the kind served in the Ginza, effete.

Iseya (tel: 3872-4886) is located at Yoshiwara Daimon-mae. It is closed Wednesdays; credit cards are not accepted.

The Pleasures of Yoshiwara

Yoshiwara, the old Tokyo pleasure quarter, is only a couple blocks from Iseya and if you're in the mood makes a colorful after-dinner walk. Although prostitution is now illegal in Japan, the particular Japanese attitude of "live and let live" has allowed what was Yoshiwara to continue in business, albeit in a different form. Where men could previously find comfort in the ministrations of high-priced Yoshiwara courtesans trained in the arts, they now go to Yoshiwara to be given a bath and sexual massage by, increasingly, women from abroad. The weekly men's magazines regularly publish photos and particulars of these women, including their prices.

The whole area is a fantasyland of flickering pink and baby blue marquees. Grecian columns of polished chromium Renaissance fountains, and plaster statues of discus throwers painted gold. Broad-shouldered young men in tuxedos stand at the doors of places with names like Mr. Dandy, Jockey Club, Star Ship, Lyons Club, Pepe Le Moko, Men's

*Club Don Juan, Shangri-la, Bunny Girl, Hole in One, Penthouse,
D-cup Collection, Baseball Club, Rolls Royce, June Bride, and La Vie
en Rose: High Society Theater. Outside of each is posted an Entry
Charge and a Service Charge, the total of which can vary from
¥10,000 to ¥50,000 and up. I suppose you get what you pay for.*

*The atmosphere here is quite different from the unabashed sleaze of
Kabuki-cho in Shinjuku, where you could get into trouble if you
allowed yourself to be set up. There is a certain dogged respectability
about the place. People living in this neighborhood seem proud of the
spectacle swirling around them and are happy to direct you to
"Yoshiwara-no-Soapland" if you get lost. And certainly, the big black
Benzes in their reserved parking places and the women alighting from
taxis in the early evening give the neighborhood a character all its own.*

Rummaging for Antiques 39

The time is long gone when you could drive into the countryside and
with a few pointed questions find a family moving from their spacious
family homestead to more contained quarters in the city, and after a
little polite bargaining bring back with you a fine old tansu excess to
family requirements for less than the price of a cheap new chest of
drawers. Now, although Tokyo has many fine antique shops (Morita
in Aoyama and Kurofune in Roppongi come to mind), they are
expensive, so the excitement of the chase is indulged in by most people by rummaging through the city's many flea markets—where,
however, there is a depressing preponderance of junk.

But Tokyo organizes itself in wonderous ways. (To buy a Buddhist
altar for the home, everyone knows you should go to a certain street in
Ueno where there are a dozen stores selling Buddhist altars; the street
is not far from the block where there are dozens of shops selling used
motorcycles.) It transpires that about 50 low-key antique shops have

somehow gathered in Nishi Ogikubo ("Nishiogi"). The shops are for the most part run by young entrepreneurs with wit, a good eye, and a genuine interest in artifacts of the past. They would be a good place to pick up something that resonates nicely with a kinder, more innocent Tokyo.

You should know that life as proprietor of an antique shop in Nishiogi is pretty languid. Most of the shops don't open until after lunch.

Nishiogi is 16 minutes out of Shinjuku on the Chuo Line. Go out the North Exit of the station and pick up a free map to the antique shops at the police box on the left side of the station.

To start, walk to the main street (known to some as "Nishi Ogikubo Kita Ginza") on the right side of the station and turn left on it. Walk perhaps half a kilometer along the brick sidewalk, across a little bridge spanning the river Zenpukujigawa, and turn left at the 7-Eleven. On this street, after the Monsieur Soleil Bakery and the bicycle shop, which will sell you all the parts you need to assemble a bicycle ("YOUR BICYCLE MADE BY YOURSELF!"), begins the procession of little antique shops, the most interesting of which are **Urban Antiques**, specializing in old silver, school desks, and park benches; **Saruyama**, specializing in old musical instruments, wooden boxes and pub glasses from the 1920s; and **Jelly-Bean**, specializing in teddy bears and framed illustrations from classic children's books.

After about half a kilometer, turn left at the Jizozaka Crossing onto another street peppered with little antique shops, the best of which are **Rakuda** ("Camel"), which specializes in wooden furniture, glass, and beautiful old bamboo blinds called *sudare*; **Jiwe**, specializing in LP records and African artifacts; and **Antiques Jikoh**, specializing in massive oak sideboards and tables.

At the fork in the street (just after "Top Sports"), bear around to the left, onto the street that will take you back to the station. Two good shops on this street are **Kinuta** and **Les Yeux Noirs**. There is also **Heartland**, a bookstore cum cafe that specializes in books about Eastern Europe and where you can choose among 20 different

Belgian beers whose empties are tucked away between the books on the shelves.

The route described will take you by most of the shops to the north of the station. There are an equal number of antique shops south of the station, but they are for the most part not as interesting.

Nishiogi is a typical suburban Tokyo neighborhood, well worth wandering around even if you are not in an antiquing mood. It is a neighborhood of flower shops, pachinko parlors, pet shops, coffee shops, barber shops, saké shops, hardware stores, candy shops, toy shops, patisseries, tatami makers, fruit stores, vegetable stores, video rental shops, and rice merchants. It is brimming over with the usual improbabilities.

Appendixes

ADVENTURE TIMES

The Little Adventures below are grouped according to approximate duration. These are just guidelines, and you may wish to allow extra time for lingering or wandering.

ADVENTURE MAP

Approximate locations of Little Adventures in Tokyo and environs. Adventures 15, pachinko, and 21, festivals, are not shown. Locations off the map are indicated by arrows.

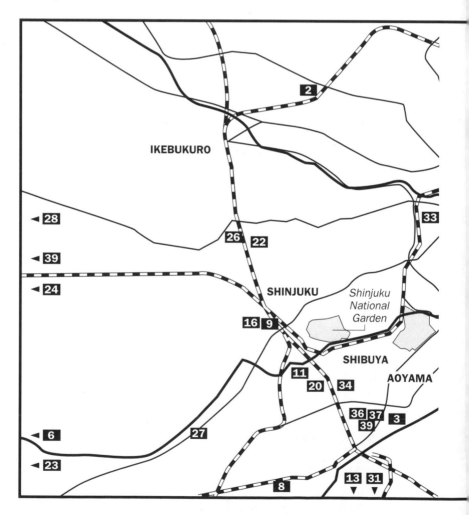

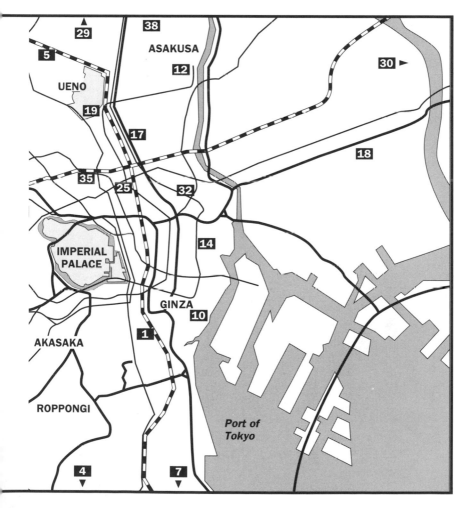

NOTES

The publisher and author welcome readers' comments
and updates on the information contained in this book.

A catalog of Stone Bridge Press books
and Japan-related software can be obtained from

Stone Bridge Press
P.O. Box 8208
Berkeley, CA 94707

FAX 510-524-8711
TOLL FREE (ORDERS ONLY) 800-947-7271
E-MAIL sbp@stonebridge.com
WEB SITE www.stonebridge.com